THE
VIETNAM
EXPERIENCE

This book is to be neither an accusation nor a confession, and least of all an adventure, for death is not an adventure to those who stand face to face with it. It will try simply to tell of a generation of men who, even though they may have escaped its shells, were destroyed by the war.

—Erich Maria Remarque, 1928
(In the Forward to his book,
All Quiet On The Western Front)

THE VIETNAM

Introduction by

EXPERIENCE

David J Bowman

GALLERY BOOKS
An imprint of W.H. Smith Publishers Inc.
112 Madison Avenue
New York, New York 10016

TABLE OF CONTENTS

Published by Gallery Books
A Division of W H Smith Publishers Inc
112 Madison Avenue
New York, NY 10016

Produced by
Brompton Books Corp
15 Sherwood Place
Greenwich, CT 06830

ISBN 0-8317-9174-8

Printed in Spain

10 9 8 7 6 5 4 3 2 1

Page 1: **An American GI in silhouette with his M16 rifle, at a base camp somewhere in Vietnam. (Photo by George Jokolai.)**
Pages 2—3: **Photos from the lives of GIs in Vietnam, 1968—69. (Upper row, first three photos from left by Ron Keil via Bill Noyes; all others by Jack Casper via Bill Noyes.)**
These pages: **US Marine Second Lieutenant JE Garney urges his men forward in pursuit of North Vietnamese Army troops during Operation Prairie II, north of Cam Lo, on 3 March 1967. (Photo by Lance Corporal SK Leighty, US Marine Corps.)**

INTRODUCTION

BY DAVID J BOWMAN

As a seemingly well-adapted Vietnam Veteran with continuous employment and a family, I had looked askance at the publicity that had arisen over the Post Traumatic Stress Syndrome. I recognize that many of my fellow veterans did have emotional fallout from the war and that a number of them suffered from broken personal and unrealized professional lives. However, the vets I saw on talk shows and news programs were not the ones I felt were representative of the great majority of veterans. I believed that most Vietnam Veterans were better adjusted and more successful than usually portrayed.

. Like many adults my age, I experienced my mid-life re-evaluation several years ago. After fifteen years in the San Francisco Police Department—including seven years as a TAC Squad (SWAT team) officer and another seven as an inspector (detective)—I decided to switch gears and go back to school. My college education had been interrupted nearly 20 years earlier by a summons from my draft board. After my Vietnam tour and Army term were up in 1968, I immediately went into the police department, but I'd always wanted a bachelor's degree. Finally, I was able to indulge myself in full-time study and enrolled in an adult college degree program.

With the concentration and appreciation few adolescents can muster, I plunged intensively into courses I had avoided or taken for granted years before. It was during the 'Great Books' seminars that I faced my own maladjustment to the Vietnam War. I was aware of a clinical coolness I possessed towards my war experience and memories. I was secretly guilty about the indifference I felt for my buddies who died. When I read Viktor Frankl's *Man's Search for Meaning* (New York, Pocket Books, Simon and Shuster, 1963), and Elie Wiesel's *Night* (New York, Bantam Books, 1982), both recounting their Nazi concentration camp experiences, my own grief and pain were suddenly unlocked and unguarded.

In his book, Frankl described three phases of a prisoner's psychological adjustment: Phase I, the period following admission; Phase II, the time of relative apathy and emotional death; and Phase III, after liberation. In these I was able to place my own war experience and understand my own frozen feelings.

Above: **Names of casualties on the Vietnam War Memorial 'wall.'** *At right:* **An American soldier in the field practices the life-preserving art of camouflage.**

Phase I: In Country

Frankl's first phase was that period following camp admission when the prisoner experienced shock and disbelief. For me, this was my arrival and first month in Vietnam. At 21 I had been inducted into the Army, trained as a combat infantryman, and sent to Vietnam. I will never forget my flight because of the airline pilot's clumsy attempt at humor when he broadcast, 'The time at Cam Ranh Bay is 0930 hours, the temperature is 110 degrees F, with the humidity at 87 percent. The field is reporting light to moderate ground fire.' It was then that I stopped denying this could ever happen to me—I had arrived in the war zone. Immediately after disembarking from the plane, the troops were sifted through multiple segregations of specialties or functions until all the infantrymen were led to a large corral where we were assigned units for a one year tour.

I was placed in the First Cavalry Division, the only 'airmobile' or helicopter-borne division in Vietnam, a unit which could stay in the field for protracted periods because all supplies and needs would be ferried by helicopter. Within 48 hours I was transported to Camp Radcliff in Binh Dinh province, the division's rear base camp near the village of An Khe. After being processed, I was advised to 'straighten out my personal affairs,' a euphemism for drawing up a will. I gave whatever worldly goods I had accumulated during my short lifetime to my mother.

The next several days were spent at the First Team Academy and refresher training in patrolling techniques and air assault tactics, followed by a UH-1 'Huey' helicopter flight to my company's forward base at Landing Zone (LZ) English near the village of Bong Son along the South China Sea. After getting my combat gear, I was flown to my unit in the mountains overlooking the An Lao Valley.

Sitting on the floor of the 'slick' (infantry slang for the 'Huey' helicopter), I watched the triple canopy rain forest below, feeling it was terrifyingly beautiful. The dense, multi-shaded vegetation screened out the sun. Occasionally, its rays penetrated and reflected a glint from an unseen source. Was it from an algae and leech infested stream, or from a weapon being turned and aimed at us? I strained to see.

The doorgunner startled me as he tapped my shoulder and shouted over the high pitched whine of the helicopter's turbine engine and 'whomp, whomp, whomp' of its rotor blades cutting through the tropical air, 'Get prepared to jump. B company is on the ridge directly ahead. They've been hit and are still drawing sporadic fire, so we're not going to touch down. Good luck, buddy!'

As I stood on the slick's landing skid, I saw a small clearing surrounded by dense vegetation. I could see figures moving about. The trees littering the clearing were not cut but splintered. I later learned that specially fused explosives, known as 'Daisy-Cutter' bombs, were exploded, spewing large pieces of shrapnel over a wide area, to make these kinds of clearings. After jumping I moved towards the company's command group, and in a clump of bamboo I noticed a man staring at me. I approached and stared back at the ashen skin, cloudy, fixed eyes, and bloodied North Vietnamese Army uniform. He was the first casualty I encountered.

The jungles were so thick that sunlight barely penetrated to the moist, organic, rotten-smelling ground. My first morning, I awoke to find the other soldiers' faces

They taught you to keep your rifle in shooting condition. *At right:* **Cleaning his M16, Sp4 Robert Canfield of Buffalo, New York, gets ready for a patrol with the 101st Airborne—in Operation Wheeler, at Chu Lai, in November of 1967. (Photo by Sp5 Ronald Delaurier, US Army.)**

covered with black shiny leeches. As I started to alert them, I realized I was probably hosting some myself. I felt my cheek and touched wet bumps of flesh. I was horrified. How could I get them off? During training I was told not to waste insect repellent. Maybe a match? But even in the daytime it was always dark under the jungle's canopy, and the flare of a match could be used as an enemy target.

'Once they have their fill, they'll fall off,' the sergeant told me calmly. 'You've got more important things to worry about.'

He was right.

After my first month in the field, my company was hacking its way through tangled vines and vegetation when there was a barrage of automatic weapons fire, followed by frantic calls of 'Medic!'

Our two pointmen were caught in an ambush. After the gunfire there was an eerie silence and I saw my first American casualties. Owen and Jim had become close friends. They were dead now, and there was no way to get them out other than by hoisting their bodies up by helicopter.

Each body was wrapped in a rubber-coated nylon poncho, and tied on a stretcher. The rotor wash from the helicopter hovering unseen above the tree line thrashed the trees violently and cycloned the ground leaves up, only to be funneled furiously downward again. In the middle of this man-made storm, we attached a nylon wrapped body to the helicopter's descended metal cable. As the cable lifted one body the waiting body's poncho flapped open. He stared skyward toward his friend being hoisted into the calm above the trees. I followed his stare. The space within yards around us remained thick and still, undisturbed by our maneuvers. I did not know these two friends in life but their deaths became an intimate part of me.

Vietnam—late 1960s: *Above:* **First Air Cavalry GI David Bowman dines in an underground bunker.** *At right:* **A UH-1 Huey comes in for a landing at a just-cleared mountaintop landing zone. The tree in the foreground was shattered by a 'Daisy-Cutter' bomb. (Both photos courtesy of David Bowman.)**

Phase II:
Rites of Passage

Frankl described this phase as the prisoner's time of falling into the camp routine. They feel lucky to have survived thus far, and do nothing to disrupt this routine, lest their good fortune run out. Both Wiesel and Frankl wrote of this period as a time of apathy or emotional death. As my weeks passed I became accustomed to more war, more death.

On 6 December 1967, just before completing my third month in country, my company returned to our base camp, LZ English, for a three day rest period after an exhausting few weeks in the field. We were to receive hot food, instead of the usual C-rations, to be allowed to shower and get clean clothes, and to be resupplied with any equipment we needed. After disembarking from helicopters, we waited on the tarmac (a tarred landing pad). Our company commander returned from the battalion Tactical Operations Center and addressed us.

'Men, we have been given a short assignment. A white bird (a Bell OH-13 light observation helicopter) has crashed nearby. We're to be inserted to provide security until the bird and its crew can be extracted.' We boarded the slicks for the short flight and supposedly brief operation.

The first couple of helicopters landed their troops in the rice paddy at the edge of the village of Dai Dong. Hostile fire erupted. All of the remaining sorties (in military aviation terms, a sortie is one aircraft trip) received ever-increasing fire while on final approach. The routine assignment had suddenly become a combat air assault. We found out later that we were surrounded by an entire regiment of North Vietnamese Army (NVA) regulars. They shot down the observation helicopter and had waited to ambush the rescue force.

We fought for what seemed like days before reinforcements could break through. As darkness fell, the NVA staged a human wave assault. They were stopped only

Above: **UH-1 helicopter troop-carrying 'slicks' in flight above the jungle of Vietnam. The door gunners on both ships have their M60s at the ready. (Photo by David Bowman.)** *At right:* **Aboard a Piasecki Shawnee transport helicopter en route to picking up wounded soldiers, Pfc David Schwinberg, of the 57th Transport Company, returns Viet Cong ground fire.**

through a combination of American firepower on the ground, and the 'Spooky,' an AC-47 gunship, that circled above us all night. It was armed with three 7.25 mm Gatling-type machine guns—each capable of firing 6000 rounds a minute. Because the 'Spooky' was painted black, and hence invisible in the darkness, it gave the illusion of thousands of descending threads of light accompanied by loud, rhythmic groaning, emanating from a black hole in the night sky.

Late that night another large force charged our position. A few of the enemy soldiers broke through the American line and were engaged in hand to hand combat. A young second lieutenant platoon leader was shot. As he fell, he was immediately attacked by an NVA. An American with a double-O buck-loaded shotgun (a high powered anti-personnel round with large pellets which is seldom, if ever, used in hunting game) fired at the NVA who was straddling the body and choking the lieutenant. Having been struck by the pellets, the North Vietnamese grinned at the shotgunner and myself, and then slumped over dead.

I turned back around and saw several NVA charging to my front. I fired my M16 and hit one. His helmet blew off as the top of his head exploded into a red mist. He staggered forward and fell in front of me.

I lay near the two dead NVA for the rest of the night. In the morning, just before daylight, I opened a can of C-rations and started to eat. As the area became lighted, I saw corpses stacked like cord-wood in front of the American positions. The bodies were covered with flying and crawling insects. I ate breakfast.

Wiesel wrote that he watched an execution and then returned to his block for a meal, adding, 'I remember that I found the soup excellent that evening.' Frankl wrote, 'The corpses near me, crawling with lice, did not bother me.'

I had entered Phase II. I was emotionally dead.

An armored column with accompanying infantry finally broke through. Together we annihilated the 7th and 8th battalions of the 22nd NVA Regiment. On 20 December, fourteen days into the 'short assignment,' the fighting ceased. Over 600 enemy soldiers were killed. Our loses were reported as 58 killed, and 250 wounded. Life had ceased to have meaning for me.

During the preparation of a mountaintop landing zone in Quang Tri Province in 1968, an Aerial Rocket Artillery (ARA) gunship was subject to small arms fire from communist troops on a nearby slope. After the landing zone was secured, the gunship's pilot, Bob Maxwell, asked if the 'friendlies' on the ground would look over his undercarriage for leaking fluids, as he made a low pass over the area. The pilot's 'foot window' had been blown out, and Maxwell himself had sustained a leg injury.

Shown *left to right, below*, is Maxwell's gunship as it made that low pass, beginning with a banking turn; then the 'short-final' approach; the arrival above the ground troops (we can see Maxwell's face through the shattered foot window); and the completion of the pass, in which we see the gunship's rear underside.

David Bowman displayed these photos at the 1986 First Cavalry Division Reunion, and a surprised voice cried out: 'Oh my god that's me!' It was Bob Maxwell, in the audience with his wife and daughter. He'd been studying his instruments when these pictures were taken, and was unaware of them.

The *above* picture was taken by David Bowman as he stood on the skid of a Huey that was on 'short final' to a mountaintop landing zone. *At left:* A UH-1 over a Vietnamese river at sunrise. (All photos by David Bowman.)

Like the victims of the Nazi concentration camps, we 'grunts' in the jungles of Vietnam had bouts of irritability, understandable in the heat, humidity, filth, and uncertainty. To combat this we developed distractions and black humor. When we 'humped' (patrolling with full packs and all equipment) along mountain trails our search patterns were, when viewed from above, in cloverleaf shapes. Since existing trails were sites for communist booby traps, they were avoided as much as possible. Our pointmen used machetes to cut their way through the thick jungle. A few steps behind them their comrades peered into the darkened forest, ready for the enemy fire that was sure to come.

The going was slow. Further back, the column waited in silence. Needing something to break the monotony and our fear, a soldier suggested that we tack signs with rhymes to trees, rhymes which would emulate the famous 'Burma Shave' signs that used to line American highways. These came to be welcome distractions, as long as the last squad removed them before moving on:

Grunts, as the slicks insert you
and Charlie does shoot at you
remember, it don't matter to you
unless a hit he does score on you
even then, it don't mean a thing to you
unless a body bag does cover you
and horizontally home they do ship you.

Then there was the parody of the Army's re-enlistment slogan:

Like hiking, hunting and camping?
Remember, you can continue to enjoy unlimited
outdoor recreation.
Just RE-UP Army today!

My year continued with the 1968 Tet Offensive. We had read that during the Battle of Hué our casualties were reported by the Department of Defense as 'acceptable.'

In April 1968 we were flown to the cloud shrouded mountains surrounding the US Marine Corps Combat Base at Khe Sanh. Our mission in Operation Pegasus/ Lam Son 207 was to make a combat air assault onto the top of the mountains that overlooked Route Nine, Khe Sanh, Lang Vei, and the Sepone River, which is the border between Laos and Vietnam. We were to engage elements of the reported two NVA divisions poised to attack the combat base. Official estimates at the time set their strength at about 20,000 men.

The mountains had been pounded for months with artillery and rocket fire, and US Air Force B-52s had also dropped hundreds of tons of bombs on the hills. They looked like a moonscape. There were large craters everywhere. Whole forests were decimated, and skeletons and parts of bodies littered the landscape. The smell of death was inescapable.

My company landed on a hilltop due south of the combat base, and we began to patrol the surrounding area of almost vertical terrain in widening arcs before returning to the hill. While we were gone, US Army combat engineers cleared the jungle and built Loading Zone 'Snapper,' an artillery fire base that would engage the communist howitzers firing at Khe Sanh from across the Laotian border.

While struggling up to the perimeter, I could not believe my eyes. Standing on the crest were uniformed military officers from many free world countries accompanied by the international press. This small hilltop had become the vantage point where the world was watching to see if this battle would be another military disaster like the French defeat at Dien Bien Phu in 1954.

At right: **A GI in a personnel carrier on an assault mission. In the background are an M60 machine gun and an M16 rifle. (Photo by George Jokolai.)**

After two exhausting weeks, the siege had been broken, and the NVA had moved on. Our company was extracted and flown to Camp Evans, a rear supply base near the city of Phu Bai. Here we were supposed to prepare for an air assault into the A Shau Valley, the supposed major supply depot for the North Vietnamese Army fighting in the northern provinces of South Vietnam.

On 24 April we made our assault into the valley by jumping onto the old French airfield of A Luoi, which the American commanders had renamed LZ Stallion. We secured the area and spread out patrolling, as combat engineers improved the runway so additional personnel and equipment could be flown in by Air Force C-130s (a four-engine medium cargo plane known as The Hercules).

Two days later, a C-130 carrying a heavy load of ammunition received enemy antiaircraft fire after descending out of the cloud cover south of the field. The pilot decided to attempt a crash landing, and was losing altitude rapidly, when he came under small arms fire. As the huge fuselage sank into the 12 foot elephant grass, only the tail fin was visible. As the tail also disappeared, an enormous yellow and orange ball of flame engulfed the airplane. The high explosive cargo it was carrying exploded for hours.

My unit was assigned the task of finding and retrieving the bodies of the crew members. After the firestorm subsided, we sifted through the charred wreckage and found small pieces of bone and flesh. As we were about to return to the airfield, I stumbled over what I thought was a tree stump. It rolled over, exposing white flesh. It was the torso of one of the crew. I carried it in my arms to the waiting graves registration personnel on the landing zone.

Immediately after returning, we were given another assignment.

Since the antiaircraft guns on hill 937 (Ap Bia Mountain*) which shot down the C-130 had not been silenced

---

*A year later this mountain became known as 'Hamburger Hill.' It was so named because of the huge number of casualties sustained by the US 9th Marines and Army's 101st Airborne Division in their 10 day battle to take the hill during Operation Apache Snow.

Much of the action in Vietnam revolved around the securing, preparation and defending of various military bases—usually located close to the enemy lines—which served reconnaissance, assault and patrol units. *Above:* Ground troops of G Company clear a mountaintop landing zone in the Vietnam jungle. *Above right:* A patrol unloads from a Huey, its door gunner with his machine gun ready to repulse hostile fire. *At right:* US Marines dig in at Khe Sanh, in March of 1968. *At far right:* US armed forces personnel man an M60 machine gun in a firefight with the North Vietnamese Army.

by aerial bombardment—and were still endangering other aircraft flying into the airfield—they had to be taken by an infantry assault. My company was one of several who were assigned this task.

We walked for hours and started up the mountain. I was one of the lead elements when I heard a terrific explosion, then rapid small arms fire. As we inched our way up the hill, I came across the body of our pointman. He had been hit point blank by a communist 37mm antiaircraft round. His head, right arm, and a large portion of his chest region were missing. I never knew his name.

Finally, we took the hill and aircraft were able to land safely from then on. The three-week invasion into the A Shau Valley, known as Operation Delaware/Lam Son 216, was terminated on 17 May 1968.

Wiesel and Frankl both described the living taking clothes and shoes from the dead. In Vietnam this was a taboo that was seldom, if ever, violated, partly because of our abundant supply, but also because we believed luck was involved with who lived and who would die. To possess equipment or clothing from a dead comrade would expose the living soldier to the same fate as the dead one.

We grunts were very superstitious and believed we would be killed either at the beginning or end of our tour. As I became 'short'—or near the time I was scheduled to be shipped home—I became very nervous. I was reluctant to volunteer for assignments and kept hoping to avoid any contact while on search and destroy missions. I did everything to protect myself. No one else mattered. I wanted to make my DEROS (Date Eligible to Return from Overseas) alive and intact.

When I had less than one week left in Vietnam, a typhoon hit during the normal torrential downpour of the monsoon season. The added rainfall flooded all the low lying areas. Since all aircraft were grounded, I had no transportation to take me to the rear for exit processing. Because we were located ten miles south of the DMZ, my company received orders to hump out of the mountains and proceed to Loading Zone Sharon, a fire base in the lowlands near Quang Tri City. There we were to provide patrolling security outside the perimeter wire of the landing zone until the weather cleared. It was raining continuously and we couldn't get over bridges or cross the swollen Song Tach Han River.

Two days after I was supposed to be shipped to CONUS (Continental United States), the rain stopped. After a short farewell to my buddies, a slick flew me to the rear.

I entered my Phase III.

At left: Troops unload from a C-130 Hercules transport. The 'Herc' could land in short, undeveloped landing zones and in adverse conditions. *Above:* Sp4 Dwight Brown, grenadier for A Company, winds up for a throw into a Viet Cong bunker while Sp4 David Perales provides cover fire with his M16.

Phase III:
Back to the World

I was rushed through exit processing and immediately flown to Cam Ranh Bay. I would later learn that I received 'special handling' because the Army did not want the publicity of having one of its soldiers killed two days after he was to have returned home.

When I was being debriefed, I felt everyone was staring at me. Only when I entered the quartermaster supply area and was fitted with a new uniform did I discover why. The new issue corresponded in size to what was listed in my personnel file, which had been prepared when I had entered Vietnam 12 months before. My 6'4" frame—which carried 210 lbs then—now weighed only 165 lbs. I was an aged youth, withered and exhausted beyond my 22 years.

Within 36 hours of leaving the DMZ, I boarded a chartered Pan Am jet for the 18-hour flight to Seattle. When the pilot announced we would be landing soon, the passengers all cheered. I was seated next to the window. When I looked down on the city below, I grew terrified.

After taxiing to the gate, everyone disembarked for the bus ride to nearby Fort Lewis and out-processing. When the stewardess told me the bus was waiting and that I would have to leave the plane, I realized then why I was afraid. It was not because of the rapid change of environment—the coming from the flooded lowlands of Quang Tri Province to the bustle of an American city in just over two days.

I was afraid of what I had become.

Living with death and destruction for so long, it did not affect me any longer. I had lived a nightmare, and it had changed me.

I returned to a society that had turned against the war, and all those who fought it. For the next several years, I tried to put it behind me—hiding my bitterness at the way I was treated. Frankl described this when he wrote, 'When, on his return, a man found that in many places he was met only with a shrug of the shoulders and hackneyed phrases, he tended to become bitter and ask himself why he had gone through all that he had.'

Thanks to Frankl and Wiesel, I now understand that my reactions during the war and to my treatment afterward were normal. Finally, I was able to cope with my feelings. I now realize I was a young man who was put into extremely stressful circumstances which I had tried to handle in my own way.

After 20 years, I finally cry for Owen C Kelley, from Missouri, and James S Kell of California, who both died in the An Lao mountains on 18 October 1967; for Walter R Boettcher, Jr, also from California, who died at Dai Dong on 6 December 1967; for Eugene A Sorenson, another California youth, who was killed on 16 February 1968, during a firefight in the village of Ton Gia Dang; for David W Casey of Pennsylvania and Daniel B Christenson from Washington State, whose lives were taken in a firefight west of Ouang Tri City on 18 May 1968; for John V Sartor from Wisconsin, and from California, Douglas D Sloan, both of whom died on Landing Zone Ann in Quang Tri Province on 24 July 1968; and for all the men whose faces and broken bodies I had seen and whose names I did not know; and lastly, for the crew members of the C-130 in the A Shau Valley, whose bodies no longer existed.

I cry for them because I had known them, their suffering, and their deaths.

Above: **David Bowman in June 1968, at landing zone Sharon, Quang Tri Province, upon his receiving the Army Commendation Medal for Valor and the Air Medal for completing 25 combat air assaults into hostile territory.** *At right and below:* **Camp Radcliff, Binh Dinh Province—the First Air Cavalry Division's base camp until January of 1968, when the division was relocated to Quang Tri Province, due to the North Vietnamese Army buildup around the US Marine Corps base at Khe Sanh. Camp Radcliff did, in fact, remain the First Air Cavalry's troop processing center until the division moved to Tay Ninh Province in late 1968. (Photos these pages by David Bowman.)**

THE CALL

After completing the basic Corps School, Michael A Wittmus was sent to the Naval Hospital at Annapolis, Maryland for general ward duty. Vietnam was starting to make an impression on his young life then. In the *Navy Times* he saw entire pages of of Navy and Marine personnel killed or wounded in Vietnam. He recalls that 'it was like having a sword hanging over your head and not knowing when it was going to fall, waiting for those inevitable orders to 'Nam.' A lot of his friends had already gone over there, and he knew he would be going soon. He was just waiting his turn.

Wittmus finally received his orders in September 1968. He had thoughts of being a photographer when he joined, but the Navy—in its infinite wisdom—made him a Hospital Corpsman (a medic) instead. To prepare him to be a combat corpsman, the Navy sent him to what they called 'Field Medical Service School'—a five-week quickie crash course on treating battlefield casualties—with a little Marine infantry tactics thrown in. The medical training was good, and it 'did turn me into a halfway competent corpsman, motivated to do just about anything for a wounded Marine.' The instructors told the corpsmen things like, 'The life expectancy of a Hospital Corpsman in a firefight in Vietnam is sixty seconds.' Wittmus recalls

that he didn't know 'whether to be proud or scared.' On the other hand, some of his training had very little to do with the realities of the type of war he would be facing.

The training took place at Camp Lejeune, North Carolina. It was November and bitter cold as they tramped among tall pine trees. It was cold as heck!

The trainees were graded on how neatly and properly they tied their battle dressings on 'fake' rubber wounds that squirted 'fake' blood. 'But they didn't tell us about the smell that went along with treating a real casualty,' he added, 'the sweet odor produced by lots of fresh blood, mixed with the pungent smell of burnt flesh and cordite, the results of a Marine being shredded by the explosion of a booby trap mine.'

Wittmus had joined the Navy because he had heard the food was good, and if he had to go to 'Nam, being on a ship might not be that bad. His mother told him not to join the Army. He would, she'd said, end up being nothing but 'cannon fodder.'

'But the joke was on me. Here I was going to Vietnam, and most likely I was going to be assigned to a Marine grunt infantry unit, as the Navy provided all medical and dental support to the Marines.'

Doug Condit was 23, a little older than average, when

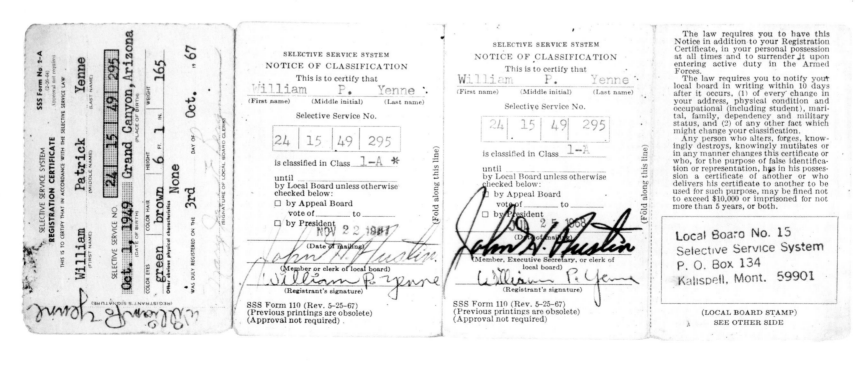

Above: Vietnam-era draft cards. *At right:* US Air Force Lt General William Momyer congratulates the crew of a C-123 Provider for heroism under fire. The crew are, left to right: Captain Richard Fritz; TSgt Charles Peterson; and SSgt William Slough. Not pictured is Captain Robert Drake.

he arrived in Vietnam. He was on a four year enlistment with the United States Navy when he was assigned to go to Vietnam with the US Marine Corps.

Before he enlisted, he had registered with the draft board in the small town of Glenwood Springs, Colorado, and had attended college for two years, with a better than average academic record. At the time he dropped out, he'd completed six quarters, was captain of his intercollegiate debate team, president of Pi Kappa Delta (a national forensics honorary fraternity), a regular actor in collegiate plays, a disc jockey at the campus radio station, and vice president of Alpha Phi Omega (a national service fraternity).

Doug Condit's only problem, like so many people of his age- both then and now—seemed to be a lack of career orientation. While in high school, he had become the Colorado debate champion (unheard of for a 'mountain kid'), but had turned down a 'Speech Arts' scholarship, as the only end he could see in this was teaching. (They did not have 'communications' majors in those days and the only 'expository writing' course taught at Colorado State University was remedial). With a love of 'communication,' but without the desire to teach, he'd decided to carry a pre-law major. However, when he took his first law course he'd become quite disillusioned because 'the lawyers who make money aren't trial lawyers as seen on TV, but those who sit behind a desk in large corporations, pushing pencils!' This was hardly what he had his mind set on, so he dropped out.

Because he was from a small town, his draft board found out, and immediately became interested in his future. To keep them at bay, Doug Condit decided to sign a contract with the US Marine Corps, which was going to send him to flight school to become a pilot. ('How glorious,' he thought, 'plus I'd get free flight training, to use either as a career, or recreation following the service.')

However, he flunked the flight physical because one of the medical corpsmen discovered that the vision in his right eye was 20/25. (It had always been 20/20 on his routine physicals, but he guessed that they must not have been as thorough.) Therefore, the Marine Corps decided to send him to Officer's Candidate School—to become a *platoon leader*!

'Nam was becoming 'hot' at that time, and the rumor was that junior officers—such as platoon leaders—lasted about 30 seconds during a firefight, so he respectfully declined the Marines' offer. They told him that he had already enlisted, so he was *obligated* to serve with them. Other recruiters told him that because he had only signed papers and not 'raised his hand' (to take the oath), he had not *officially* enlisted and was therefore free to join a different branch of the service. Condit immediately did so, and joined the US Navy as an enlisted man.

The Naval draft quota for Glenwood was only five men per month for the entire western slope of Colorado, so he enlisted in a 120-day delay program. As he had previously done volunteer ambulance work and enjoyed the excitement, he spent these four months working for a private ambulance service in Denver, Colorado. There was more than one occasion when his limited expertise was able to preserve or save a life.

'This experience—like sex—is something which is impossible to describe to someone who has never experienced it,' Condit recalls. 'I enjoyed it—though I didn't want to make it a career, due in part to the horrible pay. The owner of the ambulance service had a son who was a Navy corpsman, attached to a Marine unit in 'Nam. To hear his stories, the Marines treated him like a god—they protected him in combat, bought all his beer, etc.'

The day Condit was to leave Colorado, he was ordered

What was a covert operation in the Kennedy years became overt on 7 August 1964, with the US Congress passing the Gulf of Tonkin Resolution. *At right:* **The Ninth Marine Expedition Brigade hits the beach at Da Nang in 1965.**

to report to an induction center in Denver. While there, everyone was given cursory physicals—to make sure they were still alive—and sworn in. Because of his college education, Condit was placed in charge of the group of men that was leaving Denver that day for boot camp in San Diego. Prior to leaving Denver, one of the Naval officials there said that he could guarantee school training for five of the men prior to leaving Denver. Three of them would be schooled in electronics and two as corpsmen. The person doing the offering informed them that if they didn't get placed in a school either by him or at boot camp, they probably would end up as 'deck apes' scraping paint on ships and mopping decks. Because of Condit's previous education, he was given first choice of the five school slots offered. Condit quickly picked corpsman! While he knew that some corpsmen had to go to 'Nam with the Marines, he thought that the risk he was taking was only 50:50 at worst. If he did go, at least he already had experience as a medic—all positive.

On 9 June 1966 Doug Condit entered boot camp in San Diego, California. Following completion of boot camp, he enjoyed a two week vacation in Colorado and returned to San Diego for Hospital Corps school.

During Corps school in the fall and early winter of 1966 'Nam really heated up, and the demand for corpsmen began to increase, so upon graduation from Corps school, Condit's entire company was ordered to Camp Pendleton for FMF (Fleet Marine Force) training. When they arrived at Pendleton after FMF school orientation, he was assigned to the Naval hospital. It was an assignment that he found interesting, because it was at a Naval facility, in the middle of a Marine Corps base!

Initially, he was assigned to the SOQ (Sick Officers Quarters—though they referred to it as 'Sick Old Queers'). It proved to be a varied assignment, as he got to work with any officer who was ill—whether it was surgery, medicine, dental, psychiatric or gynecological. Condit soon got to know his own likes and dislikes.

Naturally, the senior corpsman on the ward would have been an E5—or an E4 during an emergency. However, because corpsmen were being transferred out on a regular basis, Condit became the senior corpsman when he was still an E3. Therefore, he got to be on a very friendly basis with the physicians, and requested that the Chief of Surgery allow him to obtain on-the-job training as an OR (Operating Room) technician. The Chief Surgeon had his yeoman (secretary) contact the Bureau of Medicine on Doug Condit's behalf, but 'what a shock!' recalled Condit. 'I was informed that my computer card had already been pulled and I had been reassigned. Furthermore, as this had *already* taken place and my orders—unseen and unknown, but nonetheless 'cut'—could *not* be changed.'

The Chief of Surgery asked if there was anything else he could do, as Condit's fate seemed sealed, so Condit requested a transfer to the hospital's Emergency Room, in order to refine the skills which he might apply in Vietnam.

Within a few weeks, Condit's orders came through attaching him to the Second Battalion of the 27th Marines, which were then stationed at Camp Pendleton. Following a two-week vacation, he reported to his unit in dress Naval uniform. 'What a sight!' he wrote later. 'I was issued Marine uniforms, but did not have to put up with all the BS the average Marine had to.

'The Second Battalion was an interesting unit,' Condit recalls. 'It was composed of 17-year-olds, who the Marine Corps would not send to 'Nam, until they turned 18, and of 'Nam returnees, career and others, the latter of whom were just marking days until their contracts expired and they were released from the Corps. Basically, we were a

Above right: **Mainstays of the US Air Force airlift in Vietnam, Lockheed Hercules C-130 transports deliver cargo for the US Army at Tay Ninh Air Base in April of 1966.** *At right:* **US Army troops arrive at Cam Ranh Bay in January of 1965 for an airlift, aboard the C-130s seen here, to Pleiku.**

morale-boosting/parade unit. Thus, on any given week-end, we would end up parading down the streets of San Diego or Los Angeles, to drum up support for the war effort. The rest of the time, we played with Marine toys—grenades, rocket launchers, etc—to prepare for the eventuality that the 17-year-olds would use this knowledge in combat.'

The 28th Marines were also stationed at Camp Pendleton (the 26th having already gone to Vietnam), and the two units often held massive, joint exercises with them with jets, tanks and other 'expensive playthings.'

'This was,' as Doug Condit described it, 'after all, a "play" war.'

Suddenly, on 23 January 1968, the unthinkable happened: North Korea captured the US Navy ship USS *Pueblo*. As the United States was involved in a war in Vietnam, the Pentagon had no troops ready for cold weather combat, and it was indeed reported to be cold in Korea. Consequently, at great expense to the government, the entire 27th Marine Division (with jeeps, tanks and other equipment) was flown to the mountains near Fallon, Nevada, for 'cold weather exercises.' Upon their return to Pendleton, there was an IG (Inspectors General) review, and the unit passed. The telegram went out that night: 'These men are combat ready.'

As Condit recalls, 'The following Sunday, a battalion of Marine MPs suddenly surrounded our section of the base. Those of us there had our liberty cards confiscated. Those off base were recalled. On Monday we had a massive assembly in the Mess Hall. The Colonel informed us that our unit was going on a "mount out," and while he could not tell us where we were going, the FPO assigned to us was the same as the one used for 'Nam.'

That Sunday the Tet Offensive had started. When Doug Condit called his parents to tell then that he was leaving the Continental US for overseas, he told them that 'I was either going to 'Nam for Tet or to Korea to retrieve our stolen property. We packed all of our "civies" in card-board boxes and transported them to our next-of-kin. When the postman delivered mine, he was down-hearted. It seems they used the same type of packing boxes for the personal effects of persons killed in action (KIAs).'

Condit's entire unit then was transported from Camp Pendleton, California to nearby to El Toro Air Base and flown out en masse. By the time they landed in Hawaii in combat gear, weapons at their side, their destination was not much of a secret. The air crews who ferried the unit told them that the first troops were already in Vietnam. Since they had left without officially knowing where they were going, the Second Battalion arrived in Vietnam with their cold weather gear, only to be greeted by a 80 degree heat at 2:00 o'clock in the morning when they stepped off the plane in Da Nang.

At that time, the Marine Corps had a policy that corpsmen would spend six months 'in the bush' followed by six months 'in the rear.' Upon his departure for Vietnam, Doug Condit was an E3 and senior corpsman of 'Echo' company. He had been with Echo since September, and he was promoted to E4 enroute. When he arrived, he was 'rotated' to the Battalion Aid Station (BAS) in the 'rear,' and an E5 corpsman from the 28th Marines was made senior corpsman of Echo Company.

Condit was one of only two corpsmen at the BAS who knew how to suture, and one day, as Dr Johnson was leaving the BAS for a trip, a Marine came in with a nasty laceration of his face. With a little pestering from Condit, Johnson stayed long enough to teach him how to close the laceration with a running subcuticular stitch. Although they were in combat, Condit was concerned about how the Marine would look 'back in the world.'

'Welcome to Vietnam.' *At left:* Sampans on the Perfume River in June, 1970. Peaceful-looking, but the country had been in continuous conflict since the World War II Japanese invasion. (Photo by Lou Graul Eisenbrandt.)

IN COUNTRY

Michael Wittmuss, who arrived in Vietnam in 1968, recalled that going into a village for the first time was a big cultural shock. 'What did I know?' he asked himself. 'I was just a hick farm boy from Nebraska. No one had bothered to teach me anything about the history or culture of the Vietnamese, so how could I understand them? How could I consider them more than just a bunch of "dumb gooks"? Some of the villages in the An Hoa area were in sad shape. The people lived in bamboo huts covered with old cardboard from C-ration boxes. They were filthy and living in poverty.'

Some of the Vietnamese seemed to be either indifferent or openly hostile. 'I could see the hate for us in their eyes. If there were kids yelling and running about when we entered a village, then everything was going to be all right. But sometimes it got spooky. Yet we would enter a village and it would be completely silent. We would walk around slowly and there would be nothing living in sight—no pigs, chickens, kids or people. We would search a hootch and find a pot of rice still cooking over a fire.'

Sometimes Navy medics like Michael Wittmuss would go into a village and hold sick call for the villagers, for whom medical treatment and medicine were nonexistent. They would see old men, ravaged by tuberculosis, still

These pages: **Images of Duc, a Vietnamese street vendor of soda pop, in 1969. He was all business, but where is he now? (Photo by Bill Noyes.)**

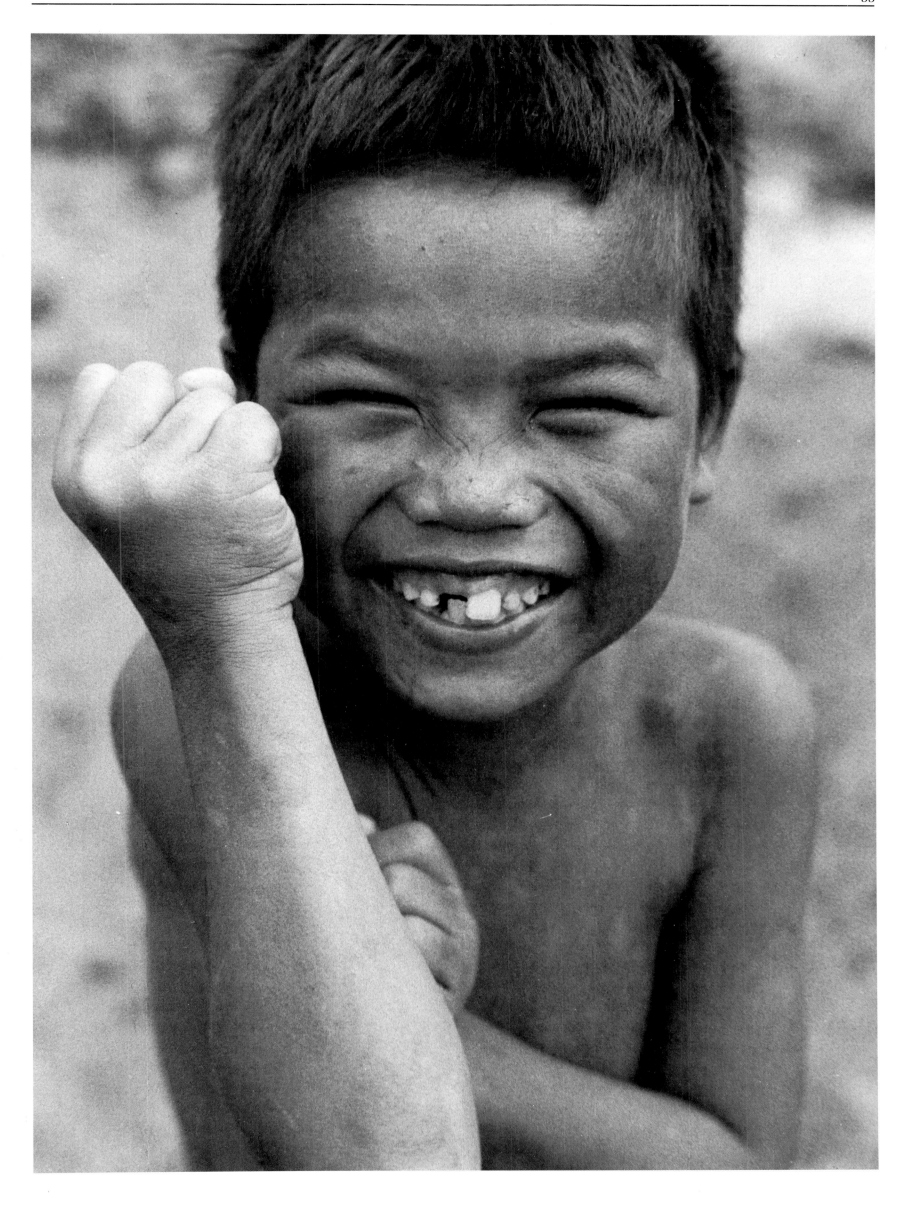

working in the rice paddies; babies with raging fevers, their heads covered with lice and scabies lesions, their bellies swollen up by some sort of intestinal worms; exotic rashes and skin diseases we had never encountered before. It all seemed so hopeless. The medics would give the villagers some aspirin or band-aids, and send them on their way.

After seeing these kinds of things for a long time, a person could get very hard and callous towards the plight of the Vietnamese people. 'We were supposed to be helping them,' Wittmuss recalled, 'but it seemed to me that a lot of these *same people* were out at night planting mines and booby traps for us to find the next day. Nevertheless, at times, we would make an all- out effort to help just one Vietnamese.'

One day, a group of excited villagers walked into Wittmuss's company perimeter yelling for a 'Bac-se' (doctor). They were carrying a small child on a board. She was a girl about five or six years old, and had a blood-soaked rag tied around her abdomen. 'When we cut the rag away,' recalls Wittmuss, 'her intestines oozed up out of a gaping wound in her stomach. It was a wound that had to hurt like hell, yet that small girl never made a sound while we worked on her. Not even a whimper. Luckily, there was a doctor in the camp that day and everyone worked frantically to save the child's life. We managed to control the bleeding, pack the wound, stabilize her vital signs and then send her out on a Medevac helicopter to Da Nang. I never heard whether or not she lived.'

That same night, the company received mortar fire from the same village from where the girl had come.

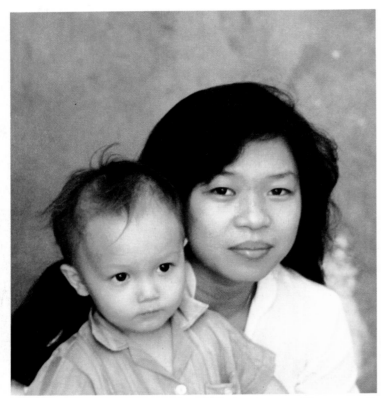

Above: **A Vietnamese mother and her child. A great many Vietnamese villagers suffered from extremely poor medical care, and the presence of the roving American military medical teams often tipped the scales against death from fever, wounds or parasites. Still, medics couldn't count on being loved for their services, and could seldom discern if they were treating friend or foe—but treat them they did. While the treatment was not always fully adequate, due to shortages of materials, it was most often all the villagers had, and it did them good. (Photo by M Heacox via Bill Noyes.)**

At right: **A roadside vendor in Hue. It was advisable to avoid purchasing refreshments from such stands, as occasionally the soda and beer were poisoned or booby-trapped. (Photo by Lou Graul Eisenbrandt.)**

Vietnam at war featured all the nightmarish illusions of war; an apparently friendly village could actually be a harbor for Viet Cong, and yet again, sometimes you thought you could read the faces around you. The shifting shadows of the war included everything and everyone—tales of seemingly innocent civilians detonating a booby trap in the midst of a crowd of GIs were all too common, and often enough, all too real. Likewise, the truly innocent frequently suffered by way of mistaken identity, and by simply being in the wrong place at the wrong time. As with all wars, it seemed the rules of who lived and died, and for what reason, were suspended.

At left: **Two girls in Vinh Long. (Photo by George Jokolai.)** *Above:* **'The Golden Girl,' a Coca-Cola seller named for her earring and false tooth, and her little friend along Highway 239 in 1969.** *At top, above:* **Vietnamese children line up for pictures while collecting 'chop-chop,' or food, from B Company on Highway 14 just south of Dau Tieng. (Both above photos by Bill Noyes.)**

Children were especially victimized by a conflict that tore families apart, both by means of systematic relocations and by the usual, more directly lethal, mechanisms of war. Children were wounded and killed like everyone else. It is especially poignant to scan the faces in the photos on these pages. The kids waiting to be fed have a sadness around their eyes—somber expressions that belie their temporal youth. They bear the mark of experience suited only to nightmares, its real context being the worst catastrophes; the grisly chaos of war. The girls' faces are touching in that they express a resilient innocence and lightness of spirit. By the cheerful fortitude of her expression, the little Coca-Cola girl shows more strength and hope than would seem possible even in a work of fiction.

Often, the only kindness that some of these children received was at the hand of the passing stranger—the anonymous faces of the military convoys, or the often under-supplied medic who gave them a simple anaesthetic before he lanced a boil, or sewed shut a weapons wound.

Doug Condit was a US Navy corpsman (medic) assigned to the Second Battalion of the 27th Marines and was expecting to be sent to Vietnam when the North Koreans seized the USS *Pueblo* on 23 January 1968. His unit was immediately deployed to the Nevada high desert for 'cold weather training.'

No sooner had his unit completed this exercise than the North Vietnamese launched their massive and bloody Tet (lunar new year) Offensive against American positions throughout South Vietnam. It was against this backdrop that Doug Condit shipped out for overseas duty in February 1968—destination unknown!

Echo Company had been in country two months when it was realized that, though the BAS was supposed to also be treating civilians, none of the medical team could speak Vietnamese. It is worth pointing out that at the time the Vietnam War started, not *one* American university or college offered a course in the Vietnamese language. Consequently, the Second Battalion decided to send one of its corpsmen to the Philippines to a Vietnamese language school. The day after he returned, Doug Condit was asked if he wanted to go to the school.

'I was no fool—a month in the Philippines? Of course,' Condit said. 'I was told to pack and my orders were cut. I went to language school all right, but instead of in the Philippines, I got to go to a language school in Da Nang, which was still a nice respite.'

The Vietnamese language school at Da Nang was run by Vietnamese in an old French fort on the South China Sea. There was a different instructor every week. As the course was only a month in length, the students were taught only how to *speak* the language, not how to *write* it. They were given a weekly test, and were informed at the start that anyone flunking a *single* test would be returned to his unit immediately. 'You would not believe all the As in that class!' Condit recalled.

In the class, Condit's assigned partner was a Marine helicopter pilot, whose time in Vietnam was running out, but who was planning to return as a commercial pilot for a reported $150,000-$300,000 salary, so he wanted to learn the language.

For five days a week, class was in session from 8 am until 3 or 4 pm. Then the American students swam with the local kids until sundown. Every Saturday they took a field trip—once going to a Vietnamese boot camp, to talk with the Vietnamese in their language. The Vietnamese soldiers in the boot camp made their rice in budge pots, and there was a Vietnamese standing in each pot, with only his shorts on, mixing the rice with a long pole and his feet. Every Sunday when there was no class and no field trip, the American language students would immediately check their pistols at the Da Nang USO and enjoy themselves in downtown Da Nang.

When he finished the language school, Doug Condit returned to his unit, where he and his fellow corpsmen began the 'Medcap' program—to go into small villages in the 'middle of nowhere' to provide medical care to the locals. They traveled with two jeeps, a radio man, two drivers and two 'shot-guns.' Even with their new-found knowledge of the language, the corpsmen found that they couldn't do too much without laboratory supplies and medications. However, they *could* clean and dress the Napalm wounds and treat abscesses, etc.

At that time, however the Viet Cong had a price on the head of every corpsman. A corpsman went into the villages knowing that if a Vietnamese could kill him, they would be rewarded with over a year's salary. Since the VC knew who the medics were anyway, Condit scraped the 'black-out' paint on his brass Cadesus insignia and let it shine. After the VC had 'visited' (hit) a village, the corpsmen would be there the next day, so each evening prior to a Medcap, Condit would shine his Cadesus, so that it would glow in the village.

'I think that the idea for "Medcaps" was a good one.

Below: Specialist First Class Sylvester Olivas with another adult and numerous Vietnamese children at a Special Forces camp at Dong Tre, in 1969. The following photos were taken during a Medcap operation at a Montagnard village in Quang Tri Province, just south of the Demilitarized Zone in 1968. *Above:* Montagnards strike a pose. *Above right:* Medic William F 'Doc' Martin with a mother and child. *Above opposite:* Villagers crowd around 'Doc' Martin as he treats a child. *Below opposite:* Infantryman David Bowman gives Montagnard children their first look at a mirror. (Montagnard photos by David Bowman.)

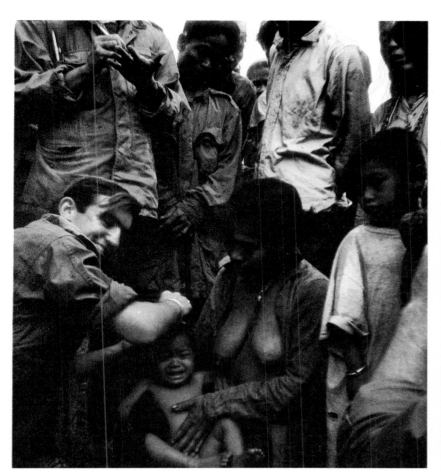

I think that we should have exploited friendship more. For example, I had this woman coming in daily for a couple of weeks with an abscess on her arm. She'd been treated by a local herb-man without results. I treated her with daily soaks and injectable Penicillin. When she was healing great (really, this had been a huge, horrible abscess and she'd been "bad-sick" with high fevers and chills), she got busted by the MPs at the gate. It seems she was trying to smuggle about a pound of marijuana—the Vietnamese knew that the GIs loved this. She was a peasant, and she was trying to show how much she appreciated that we cared for *her*. We got her unbusted, but the MPs—who were only trying to do their job and keep the Vietnamese from sneaking in pistols or grenades—confiscated her pot. (I don't know what they did with it though.)'

Condit also got a chance to visit a Vietnamese hospital, where he met a Vietnamese medical doctor who had been trained in the United States. 'They were so short of beds, they placed two Vietnamese in each bed, head-to-toe, and they appeared to *never* change the linen.'

While the Marines had to make do with old wooden and wire splints, the US Air Force in Da Nang had 'beautiful stuff,' including inflatable plastic splints. Consequently, the Navy corpsmen assigned to the 27th Marines used to visit the Air Force regularly and 'appropriate' whatever equipment they could use. Because the Air Force in Da Nang proper wasn't involved in *direct* combat and had ambulances and hospitals regularly available, 'it wasn't harmful to them.'   The same was true of rations. The Marines, who were 'in the bush,' ate out of old cans, but again, the Air Force had dehydrated food to which one simply added water. 'Needless to say,' laughed Condit, 'we appropriated it by the *case*.'

Above: **A Vietnamese boy. Some were orphans; some, simply on their own; others led comparatively normal lives; and some were pre-pubescent guerillas.** *At right:* **A Buddhist temple at Can Tho. (Photos by George Jokolai.)**

These pages: Saigon 'bar girls,' who met GIs at drinking establishments and entertained them in various fashions for tips, or favors. As often as not, a girl worked covertly for the Viet Cong. (Photos by M Heacox via Bill Noyes.)

'In Country' life: Ironic contrasts of a nation at war. *Above, at top:* A banner for a Shakespeare festival at Can Tho in 1968. (Photo by George Jokolai.) *At right:* A US Army personnel carrier winches a jeep out of the mire while soldiers, and a mother and her naked baby, look on. *Above:* Downtown Can Tho. (Photo by George Jokolai.) *Overleaf:* The advertising presented Vietnam in general, and Saigon in particular, as a truly exciting place to visit. It was, but not in the way that tourists usually think of 'excitement.' A wartime twilight zone of reality enveloped the whole area—and especially after the Tet offensive of 1968, Saigon became even more tense than it had been.

Certainly, sightseeing and tourist activities were possible, but one had to consciously choose to ignore the thickening malaise that seemed to eddy and pool in the shadows. Violence and corruption had, for years, not been more than a moment or a few feet away.

A tourist brochure proclaims: 'With its sophisticated cool resorts in highland country, white beaches, ancient imperial city, vast hunting reserves and numerous other unusual attractions, Vietnam is rapidly becoming a 'must see' for thousands of Pacific travellers... Saigon is an attractive city with wide streets shaded by tall trees. In the intervening blocks are the shops and sidewalk cafes that gave Saigon the name of "the Paris of the Orient."

'Everywhere are the street scenes that are so compelling to foreigners—the traffic jam made not by cars, but by scooters; the vendors of soup, dried meat and sugar cane juice; the fruit and vegetable mongers; the service stations for bicycles, with parts and equipment hanging around them from the trees, the doe-eyed Vietnamese girls dressed in the most gracious way....'

Another brochure describes the industrious country peasant life in Vietnam: 'A life of industry, thrift and austerity is the common lot of the Vietnamese farmer. But, despite the back-breaking toil, the Vietnamese peasant is happy and full of hope. Children work hard in anticipation of a rice cake, or a period of free time during which they can shoot marbles or fly their kites in the summer breeze....'

ENJOYING A TRIP TO THE ORIENT?
TREAT YOURSELF ROYALLY...

Visit Fascinating Viet Nam

DISCOVER VIETNAM AT NO EXTRA COST...
STOP IN SAIGON ON YOUR WAY TO HONGKONG,
MANILA, BANGKOK, SINGAPORE AND ANGKOR WAT.

SHOPPING IN SAIGON

Lacquer items, articles finished in finely crushed egg shell and pottery are the best handicraft buys. Various articles made of tortoise shell are also recommended to tourists. The Handicraft Development Center, 86 Tu Do Street, has exhibits and sales counters for Vietnamese handicraft goods. The Center also has a counter at Tan Son Nhut airport. Shops on Tu Do and Le Thanh Ton are good for lacquerware, handicraft products and shell goods.

Fun for sightseeing-shopping is the Saigon Central Market where everything is sold. Here is the place to buy a conical straw hat. Some travel agents will even recommend dressmakers to lady tourist who wants to take home a souvenir *ao dai* (the long, form-fitting, slit-sided tunic and pantaloons that make up the traditional dress of Vietnam's women).

HUNTING

Vietnam is a hunter's paradise. There is plenty of game : elephant, tiger, leopard, gaur, wild ox, wild buffalo bear, deer, pheasant. Hunting areas vary from 50 to 250 miles from Saigon. Most usual hunting bases are D i l i n h, Dalat and Banmethuot.

Highlands :
Trapping of young elephants.

Hunting season is from October to April. — As a special courtesy for foreign visitors, out of season hunting permits may be issued to them. Special arrangements may be made through the National Tourist Office, or safari tour operators. Two kinds of hunting permits will interest foreign visitors :

Licence A. — Good for big game hunting.

Fee : 4,800 VN piastres (about 68 dollars).

Licence D. — Good only for killing wild and harmful beasts such as tigers, leopards.

Fee : 1,500 VN piastres (about 22 dollars).

A royalty is levied for game actually killed : Elephant 10,000 VN $, gaur 6,000 VN $, wild ox or buffalo 3,000 VN $. Deer or bear 2,000 VN $. The owner of hunting licence A is permitted to kill one male elephant, two male gaurs, two male oxen, two male buffaloes, four bears and six deers. However, the number of wild and harmful beasts killed is not limited and there is no tax for killing them.

— 13 —

RITES OF PASSAGE

Michael Wittmuss, the photographer who became a medic, arrived in Vietnam on 18 December 1968 and was assigned to Charlie Company, 1st battalion, 5th Marines, which was located at the Marine Combat Support Base at An Hoa, about 35 miles southwest of Da Nang.

Wittmuss treated his first serious casualty—a Marine who had stepped on a mine during a mine clearing operation—within four weeks of joining Charlie Company. That's when Wittmuss discovered the 'pungent smell of burnt flesh' and the need to 'have a strong stomach to be a combat corpsman.' In medical jargon, the Marine had 'traumatic amputations of the lower extremities.' In other words, 'His left leg was blown off just below the knee, and

his right foot, which was mangled, was hanging from the bone by a thread of flesh.'

His whole body was riddled with shrapnel wounds. ('If you can picture running over someone with a lawn mower, you could achieve the same effect.') The best equipped emergency room back in the world would have had trouble keeping this Marine alive, and all Wittmuss and his fellow medic had to work with was battle dressings. It took the combined skills of two of them just to keep the bloody, mangled boy alive until the Medevac helicopter arrived. Wittmuss found out later that he had died in the chopper on the way to Da Nang. About a week after that, on the same mine sweeping operation, Wittmuss himself was wounded by a booby trap explosion.

Above: **Two F-4C Phantom crews who, on 14 May 1967, destroyed Mig-17s in combat: (clockwise from left) Major J Hargrove, First Lieutenant S Demuth, First Lieutenant J Talley and Captain J Craig.** *At right:* **'Grunts' on patrol.**

At left: Hueys come in to land in a paddy. (Photo by George Jokolai.) *Above:* Viet Cong with a captured US Air Force Airlift crewman. *At top, above:* A US Navy SEAL with a Viet Cong prisoner. (Photo by Ph1 Dan Dodd, US Navy.)

Some of the most vivid memories Michael Wittmuss has of the war are:

• Humping for miles with 60 pounds of equipment on his back, through rice paddies and up mountains in 100 degree heat;

• Spending weeks out in the bush without a bath, becoming so filthy and grungy that he no longer cared;

• Eating a monotonous diet of cold C-rations every single day for weeks;

• Hearing the heart-stopping CLACK CLACK CLACK sound of an AK-47 opening up at close range, and hearing the rounds go snapping close by his head;

• Spending sleepless nights lying in the weeds and brush of a night ambush position;

• Being eaten alive by hoards of mosquitoes and then wondering if that rustling noise he heard in the 'killing zone' was a Viet Cong sneaking up on his position—or just an errant water buffalo.

Prior to leaving for overseas, Doug Condit had been jogging five miles a day and had quit smoking for 34 months. On the flight to Da Nang, he was sitting next to a new 18-year-old Marine recruit named Thomas Rostamo.

Above: **Marines from Charlie 1/5 engage in dark humor with several South Vietnamese Popular Forces troops at strongpoint Charlie Alpha, near An Hoa in 1968 or 1969. (Photo by Michael Wittmuss.)** *Below:* **American soldiers on patrol. Hidden in such**

heavy underbrush, booby traps and anti-personnel mines were constant threats. *Above right: A US Army machine gunner leads a stream crossing, with his M-60 high and dry on his shoulder.*

'He was smoking and I smoked with him. His wife had just had a baby boy. We spent the entire flight rapping about life and death. He gave me a cigarette, and before the flight was over, I was chain-smoking. He was the CO's radio man. Although we had not been "close" in the States—he lived off-base, I lived on—we sure shared each other's lives on that flight.'

When Condit's unit—the Second Battalion of the 27th Marines—had been in Vietnam about three days, his company took its first mortalities. Two of the wounded were airlifted out and the Marines carried the third to the Battalion Aid Station in a Marine poncho. All of the corpsmen gathered around the body, wanting to see a KIA.

However, no one would uncover him.

Condit had worked on ambulances in the States and was used to dealing with dead people, so he removed the poncho, so that they could all have their sadistic curiosity satisfied. 'I was horrified,' he recalls, 'and almost threw up. It was Tom!'

Condit was on call at the Battalion Aid Station that night, and he 'stayed up the whole night with Tom's body, which was placed on a stretcher to make sure that the rats wouldn't get at it. Although his brains had been blown out, I still wanted the body to stay as intact as possible. I knew that Tom would have done the same for me. I also prayed a lot that night, although I am a professed agnostic. I went to the memorial service for Tom—the first of many I would attend in 'Nam. I don't know if the families back in the world realized the emotional services we had for the dead in 'Nam. I think we really had more meaningful services there than they could have had for their loved ones, after the bodies were returned here.

'The next acquaintance of mine to die was "Little Joe." I don't remember his last name, though I do remember his wife crying as we boarded our buses at the Camp Pendleton Marine Base. Joe also was a "new" 18-year-old, a blue-eyed blond whose hair reflected fiercely in the Vietnam sun. On his first patrol he came under attack. He hit the dirt and then raised his head to see where to fire. He was hit in the front of his helmet, and the bullet then whirled around inside of his helmet, nicking his right ear—-an immediate Purple Heart, with barely a scratch. We were all glad that Little Joe was alive and hoped that he had learned his lesson and would keep his head down. However, such was not the case. On his very next patrol, he again came under attack. This was during the 1968 Tet Offensive, the very hottest time of the war. This time, Echo Company came under attack, and when he raised his head, ever so slightly, he took a round right between his eyes.'

Above: Troops of the 173rd Airborne Division move past a fresh bomb crater. The man with the camera draped around his neck is an armed forces photographer. *At right:* A US Army platoon leader with M16 and a puppy. Note the radio man at rear. (Photo by George Jokolai.)

The Reverend Samuel L Hoard had volunteered to go to Vietnam, 'not to prosecute the war, but to take the Word of God and the Sacraments to those who found themselves serving there, whether they wanted to be there or not.'

When he first arrived in the country in May 1967, the 1st Cavalry's base camp was at An Khe. At that time, operations were mostly in the Bong Son Plains area, but the unit had just moved north to Quang Tri province in January 1968 when, in the middle of the night, the infamous Tet Offensive was launched.

Just a few hours prior to the Tet Offensive, the 1st Battalion of the 1st Cavalry Division had just arrived at its new position and had been busily engaged in the process of 'digging in' to relieve the US Marines of that particular area of operation (AO). Some elements of Marine units were still in the area when some of the Tet 'celebrators' began attacking its position, and several helicopters—which they were eager to destroy—were parked near the area.

Sam Hoard never knew whether those launching the attack were the Viet Cong or North Vietnamese Army regulars, but he did know that the enemy was pouring a lot of firepower on the 1st Battalion, 8th Cavalry's position that night, which consisted of freshly dug, man-sized sleeping holes. They hadn't had enough time to provide overhead cover, and had been able to fill only a meager number of sandbags for protection around the sides of the holes before darkness had set in.

The assault began with a mortar attack, in accordance with the enemy's usual mode of operation. When the 'incoming' mortar rounds ceased falling, everyone, except those on perimeter guard duty, thought they could relax and get some sleep. However, after an hour or so, a ground attack began. Hoard can remember vividly two Marines who set up a machine gun beside the partially completed hole into which he'd crawled. As he could see the approaching enemy's muzzle flashes from their weapons at the crest of a hill near his battalion's position, he remembers saying half under his breath, 'Praise the Lord and keep feeding that ammunition' to the Marine assisting the gunner. The 1st Battalion, 8th Cavalry got through the Tet 'celebration' with very few casualties, and successfully repelled the enemy attack.

Above: **Reverend Samuel Hoard on an operation with Company B, First Battalion, Eighth Cavalry in March 1968. (Photo courtesy of David Bowman.) Fording the often booby-trapped Vietnamese streams was a genuine risk.** *At right:* **Note this soldier's expression, as he slogs toward shore.**

A YEAR IN HELL

Reverend Samuel Hoard remembers many of the tragedies he witnessed as though they occurred yesterday: 'The many memorial ceremonies we chaplains conducted for the KIAs (men "'killed in action") of our battalion; those who unknowingly triggered booby traps left by the enemy, who had limbs or members blown off their bodies in an instant; the 19-year-old lad from Long Island, New York at the Medical Aid Station, to whose side I was called to give spiritual comfort and support, while both his legs were being amputated and he had been given only a local anesthetic; and how fear and anxiety would cause some to drink Vietnamese well water without using their purification tablets in an attempt to purposely contract hepatitis and be sent to a hospital—away, at least for a few days, from the threat of being maimed or killed by sniper fire, or a booby trap, or the dangers of becoming engaged in a firefight.

'I also remember the sense of humor maintained even in the midst of the tragedy, suffering and waste. For instance, medics and platoon leaders would go around to the different positions within the perimeter at dusk each evening, saying simply, "Ben Casey time," which was an automatic signal that all were to be reminded of the standing order to roll down all fatigue sleeves and button up at the neck in an effort to reduce malaria outbreaks among the troops. Also, whenever I was spending a night or two with one particular company—of the five which I covered—one could always tell when it was 11 pm sharp because precisely at that hour the company commander's radio telephone operator would get on the net and say to the RTO of the first platoon, "Good night, David," and the response would be a crisp "Good night, Chet."'

One night, after a bout with a sniper who had fired into their perimeter, when Rev Hoard and his friends were again engaged in more relaxed conversation, he put a question to a certain first sergeant of one of the companies: '"Top," what do you think would be the reaction of most men if they learned tomorrow that a truce had been declared and they would soon be able to go home?'

His wry reply was: 'I don't know what their reaction might be. I just know that a lot of them would have to leave their "loved ones" and go home to their wives and sweethearts.'

There was a certain amount of infidelity in Vietnam, the same as was found back home. Also to be found were the irreligious, the sacrilegious, the irreverent, the disrespectful, the arrogant, as well as racist actions, attitudes and slogans, even as they were to be found here at home. There was a lad who had printed on his helmet cover the slogan 'Kill a Gook for Christ,' and a medic—of all people—who had been routinely attending to his duties, and going about on patrols, with the skull of a human being attached to a strap, hanging from his belt loops like a

Above: Reverend Samuel Hoard, with the Eighth Cavalry in Quang Tri Province in 1968. (Photo courtesy of Steve Johnson.) The chaplain went wherever the troops had to go, including firefights. *At right:* American soldiers set up position near a Roman Catholic shrine. (Photo by George Jokolai.)

good luck charm, until one of our chaplains noticed him and had a talk with his commander, which caused the practice to cease.

In order to reach the five scattered rifle companies for whom he was responsible, Rev Hoard would start each week, if possible, by holding a religious service for the Headquarters Company in the trains (supply) area. He then traveled from company to company via the resupply helicopters on what was known unofficially as the 'Ash, Trash and Cans Runs.'

'I would remain with a company until I found an opportune time to conduct a worship service before moving on to join another one,' he recalls. 'If this meant going on a combat assault against an enemy position, or on a search mission, on a 12 kilometer march, or on a three-day operation without being resupplied, I remained with that company and accompanied them on their operation.'

Sometimes a company would become engaged in a firefight. If they suffered casualties, besides offering spiritual comfort, encouragement and conversation to try to prevent the wounded from going into shock, he would also assist the medics. It was helpful to the medics for him to be there to slit open the sleeve on the fatigue jacket of a seriously wounded man so that the medic would have quick and easy access for administering morphine, if it was needed. The chaplain also assisted in moving the wounded to designated points where medical evacuation choppers would land.

Having a former classmate who worked for a Lutheran radio station back home in St Louis, Rev Hoard had been asked to send back taped interviews from some of those members of the 1st Battalion, 8th Cavalry who happened to be of his faith. Some of the big questions he'd ask were: 'How do you feel about being engaged in this war, so far from home, and how do you feel about the demonstrators against the war back home?'

Their answers varied somewhat, but most were generally of the same vein. The soldiers believed that the demonstrators should be entitled to freedom of speech, but not when it gave aid and comfort to—and abetted the cause of—the very enemy with whom they were engaged in battle and who were threatening their lives and killing their comrades.

Despite the war, some GIs kept a sense of humor, like the Marine *above*, circa 1967. (Photo by Rob Jenkins via Bill Noyes.) *At right:* **Army engineers, emplaced with their hammocks. (Photo by Jack Casper via Bill Noyes.)**

People would frequently ask Rev Hoard how he felt about his country's involvement in the war and about his own personal involvement. At that time, his answer was always threefold.

'First of all, young men from all elements of society were being drafted for this war—from your neighborhood and from mine, from your race and from mine, of your religious faith and of mine—from *our* country. Not all opted to go to Canada or to jail. Therefore, I resolved that I was in the Reserves to serve when needed. Chaplains were needed to take God's Word and the Sacraments of the church to our troops in Vietnam.

'Secondly, it was hard for me to give an answer to all the various questions on the morality and conduct of the war in general. I had to admit that the people back home probably knew more about the overall picture than I did because they had instant coverage on various aspects and the conduct of the war throughout the country via the media and television. I could only speak about the operations I was a part of and of the people we encountered where we were. However, I could attest to the fact that the Vietnamese people were constantly supplying our troops with intelligence on the communist enemy forces who were harassing their villages. The villagers were exuberantly grateful to us when we would repel—or eliminate from their area —those enemy forces who were unjustly confiscating their hard-earned harvests of rice for Viet Cong or NVA use. The American forces had regular supply lines. Hot meals were flown to us daily by helicopters, when operations permitted. We certainly did not want, nor need, their harvests, as the North Vietnamese did.

'Thirdly, as to the question of whether or not I felt our forces should have even been in Vietnam, my answer was always conditional. I believed that as long as powers from the North were infiltrating the South and trying to force their philosophical ideologies upon the South Vietnamese, even at gunpoint, and as long as our forces had

A study in contrasts. *Above:* 'Tunnel rats' in 1967, on a search mission to uncover items used by the Viet Cong in training their recruits in installing and camouflaging booby traps. This is as 'ground level' as war gets. On the other hand, *at right* are personnel of the 64th Fighter Interceptor Squadron scrambling to intercept an invader with their F-102 Delta Daggers, in 1966.

At left: ARVN (Army of the Republic of Viet Nam) soldiers and a captured Viet Cong in 1967. It's a treat to air your feet—*above*, 502nd Infantry Sergeant James Brusso wrings out his socks as Sergeant JD Harrell rolls a smoke, at Dong Ba Tinh, in July, 1965. (Photo by SP4 Dennis Thompson, US Army.) *Below:* US Marines traverse a patch of wildflowers—good cover for mines or an ambush—south of Da Nang. (Photo by LCpl Brusch, US Marine Corps.)

been invited by the official South Vietnamese government to assist them, we were right in being there.

'Anyone who does not believe that atheistic communism and its proponents do not present a threat to the ideologies of democracy is entitled to his or her opinion,' said Reverend Sam Hoard, 'but that opinion does not jibe with mine.'

The procedure at a Marine Corps Battalion Aid Station called for the sick or wounded to be registered and then be seen by one of the US Navy corpsmen. Less than 10 percent of the patients were referred by the corpsmen to one of the medical doctors. The corpsmen provided 'basic' health care. On days when the battalion was being airlifted to a 'real' battle, corpsman Doug Condit of the Second Battalion of the 27th Marines recalled that 'we might have 200-300 Marines show up "sick" at 8:00 am and have to triage them. What a bummer! We knew that some of the Marines to whom we gave cold tablets and sent out were probably sick, and that some of the others, who we gave "sick" chits to—so they could remain in garrison—were probably malingerers. But we did the best that we could under the circumstances.'

According to Doug Condit, the equipment supplied to the Marines 'was the worst. We had some nice stuff from CARE, with the instructions that it was supplied by Americans for use on *Vietnamese only*! Well, to hell with that! We rationalized the use of this equipment on the Marines by saying that we were using United States military supplies to treat Vietnamese and military people, which had been paid for by American taxpayers, like the parents of the men we treated.'

A Marine Corps Headquarters company included the aides (secretaries,) communications men, and so forth, along with the Battalion Aid Station (BAS). However, Headquarters did, on occasion, run daylight reconnaissance patrols near its base— often with a corpsmen present. Although the corpsmen went as 'volunteers,' it made for a change of routine. There were also night reconnaissance patrols, again with corpsmen only as 'volunteers,' and Doug Condit was a not infrequent volunteer. 'The night patrols could really scare you though,' he recalls,

Douglas Condit, Jr was with the 27th Marines and the 7th Engineers in Vietnam, in 1967—68. He is shown *above* on the steps of a Battalion Aid Station, which he describes in the text, this page. (Photo courtesy of Douglas Condit, Jr) *At right:* Soldiers of the 173rd Regiment patrol a rice paddy.

'because when it got dark in 'Nam, it got *really dark*. Our battalion patrolled the 'rocket-belt' 24 miles south of Da Nang. For Da Nang to get hit, we had to be hurting—I mean hurting!'

One night, for example, Condit's patrol was watching the main road coming into the compound. 'It was ours during the day, and the VC's, during the night. But the VC wouldn't play fair. Besides transporting their equipment all night, they would often plant a bomb in the road during the night as a surprise for us in the morning. Consequently, we had engineers attached to our unit who would sweep the roads for mines every morning.'

This night, the patrol took two infra-red scopes and set up a position along the road. They left after midnight, so they wouldn't be noticed, and were back at sunrise. They were just spending the night along a deserted segment of road—not walking or moving. There were two Marines looking through the infra-red scopes at all times, so Condit dozed off. The next morning, the engineers swept the road and found nothing. Condit and the Marines hadn't seen anything during the night, either, but the first truck hit a land mine not 50 feet from where they'd been positioned. It was blown to bits.

A few days later, 2d Battalion got a call that some engineers had tripped a booby trap alongside the same road. Doug Condit and Dr Jim Johnson climbed into the BAS jeep—which doubled as an ambulance—and sped to the scene. The Marine with the most serious injury was 500-1000 feet from the road. 'As Jim and I ran through the underbrush toward him, the Marines hollered at us to not run next to each other; in case one of us tripped a mine, the other would be available to treat him. Talk about vulnerable!'

When they reached the Marine who had tripped the booby trap, he was lifeless. They placed him on a stretcher, and started CPR. 'It was odd,' Condit observed, 'that we could see no wounds. We sped his body back to the BAS and placed him on a table. When we stripped him, the only injury we found was a small 2mm cut next to his navel, yet we couldn't revive him! Though they never

At right: **Two Marines of the Third Battalion, First Marines, investigate a Vietnamese hut in Quang Tri during Operation Badger Tooth, in January of 1968.** *Above:* **Members of the 503rd Infantry confiscate sacks of rice found in a Viet Cong cache near Bong Son. (Photo by Sp4 Larry Gillis, US Army.)**

learned whether the Marine ever had an autopsy, all they
could guess was that a tiny piece of shrapnel had lacer-
ated his aorta.

For a period of about three weeks prior, the unit had
been on constant 'red-alert' every night. However, on
none of those nights did the enemy strike. One night, at
bedtime, as he was undressing, Condit decided that his
feet were rotting off from sleeping in his boots and that he
was going to sleep comfortably for a change. The other
corpsmen agreed, hooted and hollered and stripped.
That night, they were hit with a barrage of Russian
122mm rockets. The corpsmen hurriedly dressed and
went to the BAS, where there was a bunker large enough
to treat two Marines. It was overflowing, and in the
rockets' red glare, they could see more and more wounded
Marines being carried in. Naturally, the camp was in a
blackout condition, so Condit went to the rear of the BAS
and fired up the emergency generator, lighting the whole
area, amid screams from the other corpsmen to douse the
lights. But it was too late. The camp was under siege for
48 hours and the corpsmen worked continuously, remov-
ing shrapnel from every place imaginable. Marines with
minor shrapnel wounds were asked to return in four to
nine hours to have the shrapnel removed. Dead Marines
were placed in body bags and stored out back.

The troops in the field could listen to one of two radio
stations—the Armed Forces Network or Radio Hanoi.
Radio Hanoi always spoke personally—they would say
'hello to Second Battalion'—and they would also broadcast speeches by people like Jane Fonda.

'They knew how to get us depressed,' Condit recalls.
'While we knew that what Radio Hanoi was saying was
propaganda, we also realized that what the US govern-

Above: **A wounded Viet Cong infiltrator and a Viet Cong nurse—after surren-
der to ARVN Rangers, following heavy street fighting in Cholon in June,
1968. (Photo by Sp5 JF Fitzpatrick, US Army.)** *At right:* **Soldiers of the 15th
Cavalry man a 105mm howitzer at Fire Support Base Anna, in 1970.**

ment station said was more than likely censored. In the evenings, at one of the clubs, we would sit around and ask each other why we were there. I had rationalized my position. I explained that as long as Americans were there, fighting and getting wounded, I indeed had a reason for being there, as an individual. However, I was questioning the morality of the war even then—as were most of the Marines.

'All of a sudden, word came down that the 27th Marines were being returned to the States. Rumor was that the Second Battalion was not even supposed to have gone to Vietnam, that it had just been a weekend screw-up at the Pentagon. We should have gone to aid the USS *Pueblo*. If anyone ever knew how or why we got there, it is beyond me. The corpsmen were given an individual choice: either return with Second Battalion to Pendleton, or finish out our year in 'Nam. If we elected to return to the States, we would *not* be credited with having been to 'Nam at all (although we could keep our medals), and if we had a year or more on our contract, we could expect to be *returned* to 'Nam, for a *full 12-month tour*! However, if we elected to stay in 'Nam for the remainder of our year, we would be reassigned to "rear," non-grunt units for the remainder of our tours. *Tough decision!* I elected to stay.'

No sooner had Condit volunteered to remain "in country," than the Chief Surgeon took all the corpsmen who elected to stay and put them with line companies and returned the corpsmen from the line companies to the BAS for transfer back to the States. They never knew why.

Thus it was that Doug Condit became senior corpsman of 'Hotel' Company. As the senior corpsman, he had to accompany the 'headquarters' part of the company on operations and had the responsibility of assigning seven other corpsmen to various platoons.

When Doug Condit arrived at Hotel Company, they had the hottest area of the Second Battalion's scope of coverage. (Company assignments were rotated between hot and not-so-hot areas on a regular basis by the battalion brass.) The area Hotel was covering included the village of Duc Khe, which was universally known by its phonetic interpretation—Duck Key. It was the same area where Thomas Rostamo had been killed. Although that had been several months earlier during the height of the Tet Offensive, they still couldn't send out a patrol without encountering trouble.

One day, one of the patrols got pinned down in Duck Key. The executive officer of Hotel Company got some extra troops together and they all boarded Amtracks (M113 Armored Personnel Carriers). For them it would be a short, motorized ride, while the initial patrol had taken three days to reach Duck Key. Their arrival was greeted

Above: A search-and-destroy unit of the 173rd Airborne Brigade checks the vicinity of a bomb crater for Viet Cong activity in War Zone D, in 1966. *At right:* Soldiers of the Fifth Mechanized Infantry on a line of attack during Operation Kalamazoo in April, 1966. (Photo by Sp4 Bill Vickery, US Army.)

by mortar fire, but unless someone was unfortunate enough to take a direct hit, the damage was minimal.

Doug Condit grabbed a foxhole with the company's radio man.

'He left me alone and went to rap with a buddy,' Condit remembers. 'While he was gone, for the first time in 'Nam, I was responsible for the death of a couple of Vietnamese. Along the perimeter where my hole was, I suddenly saw two adult Vietnamese males (about 25-35 years of age) appear from the bush and start running away from our area. I immediately sounded the alarm and Marines came out and began firing at them. We were in a free-fire zone, and thus able to fire without asking questions at these two running targets. It was kind of like deer hunting, but these were human beings. It gave me a very eerie feeling. I don't remember if the Vietnamese had guns or not, but if they had been innocent, they should have walked toward us, arms in the air.'

Several days later, Condit's patrol found a civilian woman, about 30, who had just triggered a booby trap. One of her hands was maimed, and part of her guts were hanging out. He arranged for medevac to a helipad by truck and to Da Nang by helicopter. 'In my own mind,' he recalled, I always wondered *why* she triggered a booby trap. Could she have been setting it?'

When it came time to care for her, though, he gave her prompt, correct medical attention—an IV, the whole bit—although he was 'as paranoid as anyone else while in 'Nam.'

Near Duck Key, on one of the occasions when he'd gone with a patrol to bail out a unit in trouble, one of the Hotel Company corpsmen—we'll call him John Doe—had an acute 'situation reaction.' The corpsmen were divided in groups of two to a platoon. Each platoon had three squads, and each squad had about 12 men. When they went on patrol, one squad (usually with the platoon leader) would remain 'set in' a central point. At various times of the day or night the other two squads would run patrols from the center. One squad would run a short patrol, the other a long patrol. To provide adequate medical coverage for all three squads, one corpsmen would stay with the one that was 'set-in' and one would go on the *long*

The face *above* could belong to a Viet Cong saboteur. *At right:* Long Range Patrol personnel of the 151st Ranger Infantry, behind enemy lines—left to right, scout Duong Van Than; patrol leader Sergeant James Wicks; and senior scout observer Sp4 Salvador Romero. (Photo by Sp4 Richard Goff, US Army.)

patrol. Often, the corpsmen would vary who did what, but each particular corpsman always stayed with a certain squad of his assigned platoon.

On the day that John Doe 'freaked,' the last Marine—of the 12 that were there when he joined Hotel—had died in his arms. (While not all of them had died, all had either died or been medevaced.) John Doe's platoon had 24 hours remaining on patrol and Doug Condit was faced with deciding whether to send him back to base, medevac him, or require him to stay with his unit. Condit rapped with him for quite some time and tried to comfort him as he cried, and allowed him to vent his feelings. Condit then told him that he would rap with him more the following day—when they got back into garrison after the patrol. John Doe did finish the patrol—'for which I am grateful—and hope that he is too,' Condit said afterward. 'I was afraid to take him out after that because I did not know if he would ever be able to return to a combat situation again and/or how he would face himself in the future. It's kind of amazing to me that young, non-career people have to make decisions like this. If he would have been killed or wounded during the next 24 hours, I have no idea how I would feel now. Since he *did* make it, I think that my decision was right. It's hard to argue with success. Yet, had those 24 hours ended differently... '

Shortly after Condit's arrival at Hotel, the company got a reprieve. They were reassigned from Duck Key to guard a bridge between the Second Battalion headquarters and the regimental headquarters. It was the summer of 1968 in Vietnam and it was extremely hot and extremely humid. When the company arrived at the bridge, the company CO asked him about the health prospects of allowing Marines to swim in the water. Condit replied that he would 'imagine that the Division Surgeon, if asked, would prohibit swimming in the river.' The water was black. The Vietnamese peasants did not have restrooms, and it was not unusual to see dead animals, or portions of them, floating down the river as well.

However, Condit told the CO that 'swimming in the river would boost the troop morale, and might be a nice change after Duck Key. I suggested that we place our shower facilities next to the river, so that the Marines could swim and then wash the excrement from their

At right: **American advisors (left and right) Sergeants George Hoagland and Richard Pegran discuss assault strategy with ARVN personnel, in the Central Plateau Region in 1964.** *Above:* **Protected against Viet Cong by American GIs, Vietnamese farmers harvest their rice in Phu Yen in 1966.**

bodies. The CO bought the idea and the Marines swam.'

Some nights while at the bridge, when there were reports that the enemy might try to capture it, tanks would be positioned at either side. On one of these nights, 'one helluva lot of North Vietnamese regulars crossed the road in front of one of the tanks (over 100 yards away, but in front),' Condit recalled, having been in the tank at the time, looking at the men as clear as if it were day. Yet the tank men could *not fire* at these NVAs, as there was a South Vietnamese Base at a far end of the road.

When the Second Battalion was finally relieved of 'bridge duty,' it became an 'extra unit,' available at the whim of the top brass. One night, for example, they were told that at daybreak they would be taken to a valley by helicopters for an all-day search and destroy mission. As it was hotter than hell, Condit lined up all the Marines in Hotel Company and force-fed each of them two salt tabs and a canteen of water. (Another company had just taken over 70 percent casualties on a mission due to heat exhaustion, and he didn't want the same thing to happen to Hotel Company.) In what came to be regarded as typical form, the operation was canceled just as the unit was lining up to board the helicopters!

Just prior to the disbanding of Second Battalion, the entire unit was sent on a three day search and destroy mission to an area just outside of Da Nang near Monkey Mountain. The area was loaded with booby traps which the Division brass wanted destroyed. Mine detectors and other equipment which the unit had were loaded into trucks. Enroute, one of them—loaded with Marines—was blown up by a land mine. The casualties were medevaced and there were no immediate deaths, but shortly after the mission had begun, it began to rain, so that the mine detectors became useless. The first night the men slept standing up in three feet of water, in a constant downpour. The second day, as the battalion was plodding through monsoon-like rain, about 100 yards to my left

At right: **An engineering unit salvage operation for an M48 tank damaged by Viet Cong explosives near Pleiku, during the Tet Offensive in 1968. (Photo by Lt Jack Casper, via Bill Noyes.)** *Above:* **A weary soldier after intense fighting.**

bodies went hurtling into the air. Some of our Marines had found a mine.

The man who had triggered the mine had obviously done so with his hand, as all the flesh had been ripped from his fingers—an instant skeleton. It had also shredded his common femoral artery and vein. Doug Condit reached him, but found there was no place to put a tourniquet or clamp to stop the blood flow. The rain continued to pour down, and the wind was blowing very hard. There was an air controller with the unit, whom Condit asked to radio Da Nang for a medevac helicopter for the three Marines. He radioed but he was told that everybody was grounded. Condit asked for volunteers, and told the unit that the first Marine was dead and one of the others would probably die without emergency care within 60 minutes. He got the volunteers. Though they had to carry the dead Marine out with them, a medevac helicopter did come—with a gunship escort—within 10 minutes. The helicopter didn't totally land, it just hovered over the water-filled rice paddies, as they loaded the two wounded Marines. The pilot had a great deal of difficulty taking off, but he made it—and both of the wounded Marines survived.

Finally it was morning and the weak rays of sunlight were chasing the night's shadows from the berm line road. The sun shone through the even-spaced rubber trees behind the bunker line, reaching the soil in spots, and a light breeze sometimes rustled the placid foliage. Now the corpses lay scattered in fleeting shadows brushed by the glimmering light. They lay as they had fallen the night before, already frozen by death. They'd

Below: **A 173rd Airborne Brigade trooper takes cover as air support lays waste to the enemy's position, in Operation Junction City. (Photo by Sp4 Paul Epley, US Army.)** *At right:* **A GI of the first US Army combat unit in Vietnam, with hand-rolled cigarette and shredded fatigues, in 1965.** *Above:* **Rifle cleaning.**

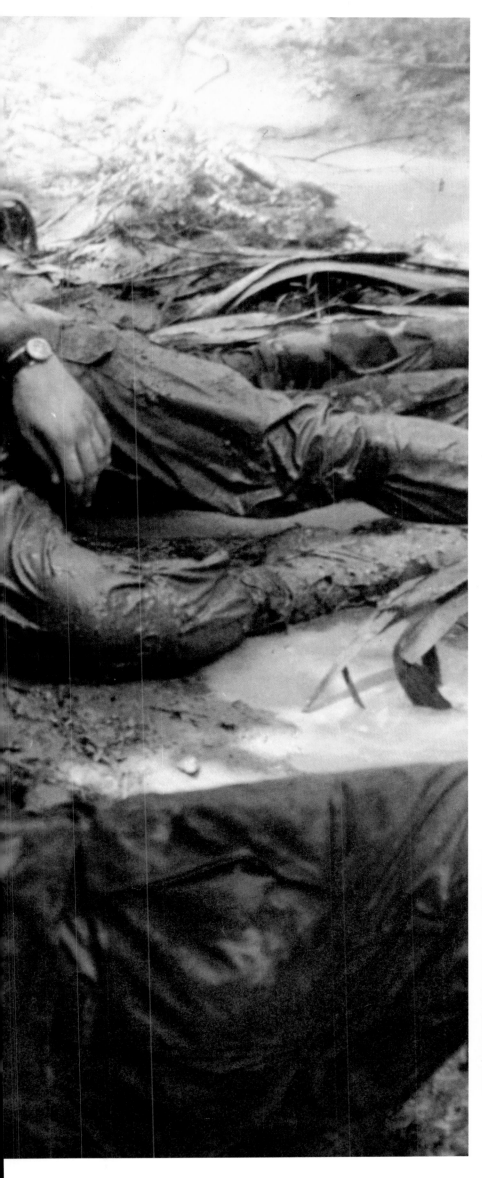

breached the wire, blown the bunker and hurried to cross the road to enter the trees. The stillness was receding with the shadows as Bill Noyes stood above the enemy sappers, looking at a dead American. He and his comrades were survivors of the garish night, caught in transition to a bustling new day.

'We were the twenty-three members of the 3rd Platoon. Part of the mechanized reaction force for the base camp at Dau Tieng, we had been separated from Bravo Company early in the long night. At the start of the NVA's assault, we had waited in the 2/22d battalion area several miles away at the opposite end of the base camp. In cautious starts, we made our way down black streets, across the airstrip and into the area of the camp that the enemy had overrun. Our three trucks had rumbled behind us as we felt our way with our rifle muzzles through the darkness, not knowing either the area or where the enemy might be.'

The battle started with a sudden mortar barrage. Noyes listened to the firing and the rockets landing at the opposite side of the base. The sector seemed strangely quiet. Not noticing much activity in the floating flare light there, the troopers worried that their bunker line—that was about 100 yards behind—was poorly manned. Because of standby orders, the tracks idled on the open street to the front of them as the soldiers readied their equipment. They watched the tracers fly from the far end of the darkened base camp into the sky and into the tree line of the Michelen rubber plantation, which was barely visible beneath artillery flares.

The battle seemed a distant, picturesque spectacle until they heard the soft, slow slicing of mortar rounds falling through the night air. The barrage landed with rhythmic crashes along the roadway not far away, the bursts methodically stepping toward the tracks. 'Fragments cut the air and landed with thuds as we scattered and scrambled into hiding. Then, only a dust cloud was left to merge with the night.' No one hurt, the immediate danger vanished with the sound. 'We were part of the battle now, more anxious to be moving than before,' Bill Noyes recalls.

And the word soon came: 'Move out!'

As they rode the rumbling tracks down the dirt street toward the airstrip, the relay of talk from the platoon leader's track said they were going to outpost some artillery. The mission somehow changed as they approached the dark airfield. 'We were to cross the airstrip, but the question was, how?'

In the darkness the airstrip was an unknown obstacle—a solid, black 'kill-zone' to be breached. A whispered conference was held at the lead track: 'Exactly how and by whom?'

That there was danger, it was agreed. They knew some

At left: **Sp4 Jim Messengill, of Ranger Troop H, 75th Infantry, reports contact with the enemy northeast of Xuan Loc, in December of 1970. (Photo by Sp4 John Skiffington, US Army.)** *Above:* **Sp4 Robert Chestnut, of the Fifth Special Forces Group, calls in a position report near An Khe in 1969.**

enemy were past the bunker line and into the base. Two spotter planes had been destroyed on the runway. Their fear had thoroughly mixed with the blackness before them when Bill Noyes and two other trooperss—all veteran infantrymen—began a determined rush across the void.

'Our magazines tugged at the straps across our shoulders and around our waists with each running step. Their weight was felt in the knees, and the hardness of the ground at each pounding footfall. Their slap and rattle, a throbbing heartbeat in each ear, were the dominant sounds of this quiet reckoning to the crossing. Behind us, more footsteps started; ahead, there was only silence.'

The ditch along the opposite edge of the runway took slow form at their approach. 'The night was now warm with sweat. Then we were at the ditch's edge, blackness inside, darkness surrounding it. Crumb was the first man in, almost disappearing. We followed. All waited, crouching, as the shadows around us loomed larger and the track engines surged in the darkness beyond.'

As the platoon collected, they discovered two frightened figures further down the ditch, one slightly wounded. They'd met the sappers earlier and they told their story excitedly to the four or five troopers who'd just arrived. They felt lucky to be alive and glad at this friendly meeting in the dead of night. The visit lasted only a short while before the platoon resumed its push into the unknown, gingerly probing past vacant bunkers and buildings, a blind march to the Wolfhound sector of the bunker line.

At some black spot in the darkness, the lieutenant turned them to the left and, shortly, they broke from total darkness into a scene of weird, shimmering shadows and the chaos of a battle that seemed nearly ended. Bill Noyes and his platoon found themselves at the bunker line where the Wolfhounds had been overrun by sappers. 'In the rocking flare light, the men's wild, frenzied eyes glinted and shone with the tension of the night's battle. Their exhaustion gave way to obvious gladness at our arrival, as our tracks drove on line between the bunkers. We could see no enemy fire from the shadows in front of us as we dismounted and readied for firing. The Wolfhounds pointed with vehemence to where the enemy had been in the dark. The tangle of shadows and concertina wire awaited our attack.'

Above: **A 28th Infantry soldier clears underbrush for a landing zone in 1967. (Photo by Sp4 Alan Showalter, US Army.)** *At right:* **Troops of the 25th Infantry prepare to patrol the Michelin Rubber Plantation, as elements of the 34th Armor provide cover. (Photo by Pfc Richard Sanders, US Army.)**

The trooper's .50 caliber fire erupted, mixed with rifles, machine guns and grenades, and with the cheers of the Wolfhounds. 'We raked the ground, our tracers bounding into the blackness, darting between each wire post. After the firing, the boisterous yells and cheers faded more slowly. The tracks roared while backing off the bunker line and we turned to leave this eerie, junk-strewn place. Some Wolfhounds bid us a clenched fist and V-sign goodbye, their calls showing their spirits had been raised. Quickly, we were back in the enveloping darkness.'

Mounted high on the tracks, scanning each black opening or crevice in the darkness below with weapons ready, they rode in slow progress through the night. They clanked along a mysterious street and roared onto the airstrip again at its lower end, then followed the gently rising strip along the familiar ditch until they reached the middle of the runway. Here they stopped and waited, the camp hushed all around them.

From the idling tracks they could see the dawn sky graying above the distant plantation tree line. Across the airstrip were the dark, blasted hulks of the aircraft the sappers had destroyed. A single body lay crumpled on the ground. Some in the platoon had dismounted and attempted to sleep, their weapons close. The tracks shut down. They waited in the dark quiet, but only for a moment. 'Mount up!' and they were moving again!

The platoon headed down the central camp road and soon came to the old two-story plantation house. In the roadway they found a jeep and a truck stopped. Their drivers lay to the side. 'We rumbled closer,' Bill Noyes recalls. 'The men were not dead, but moving. Suddenly, several bullets ripped through the air around us. There were snipers in the old house! We were airborne with this realization, feeling the weight of our weapons and the

Above right: **A bomb strike in August 1971.** *Below:* **A bombed-out house and sometime sniper's nest, evidencing several waves of weapons damage. (Both photos by Doug DeLay via Bill Noyes.)** *Below right:* **Abandoned houses like this were often sniper's nests. (Photo by M Heacox via Bill Noyes.)**

ammunition even before we landed, hard, in the dusty road.'

More shots flew past as they scrambled into the ditch along the masonry wall that lined the plantation manager's yard. While most huddled close to the ditch bottom, several others sprang up in succession to return fire. They fired for an instant, sometimes emptying their magazine at the buildings, then returned to the safety of the ditch to reload. Up again, another magazine gone, then down, quickly engulfing the roof and windows in gun fire.

Then the yelling of the men behind the jeep told them to cease fire, claiming that there were friendlies on the opposite side assaulting the house. So they lay in the dust and waited while the assault progressed unseen.

After a few minutes, without any more shots coming their way, they were again ordered to board the tracks and move out. Unsure about the enemy in the house, they watched it closely, expecting bullets as a send off as the tracks rolled quickly past and down the road. None came, and they left the plantation house in the morning grayness and dust.

Approaching an intersection further along—Highway 14, which ran between the north and south gates—the platoon pulled over to the side of the road and stopped. Coming from the direction of the north gate, adjacent to the Wolfhound's sector, two trucks and a jeep appeared in the thin light and crossed in front of them. 'Jungle-booted feet of corpses were revealed as they sped past going, no doubt, to the medical facility for processing. The small procession passed without response from us. We watched as experienced, but confused and embarrassed, witnesses fixed to our machines, awaiting further directions.' Soon the orders came. The tracks clanked around the turn which led to the south gate.

The news via radio had become tangled and vague as it spread through the squads atop each track. They were to 'replace the guards who fled the bunker line in the engineer's sector.' They'd been overrun, the number of enemy was unclear. The troopers worried about the stories of a massacre at the PX and the hospital, and doubted them also. It seemed that setting the situation straight was the mission of the Third Platoon alone. 'Questions and complaints were our meek response to the orders. The choice, however, was not ours as the tracks obediently took us forward in the dim morning light.'

Past the turn a short distance down the road lay an American corpse in flack jacket and helmet, sprawled next to a burned fuel storage bunker. 'We all looked at him in passing, struck by his peaceful solitude amongst

At left: **With an M113 armored personnel carrier for cover, a squad of the 11th Armored Cavalry patrols near Long Binh, in February, 1969. (Photo by Sp4 Kenneth Powell.)** *Above:* **Pfc Charles Holland (with M16 rifle) and Pfc Joseph Long (with M79 grenade launcher) at Bien Hoa Air Base in 1965.**

the trees that lined the deserted avenue. Continuing in the colorless morning light, we turned before reaching the main gate to follow the berm line road.'

As they rolled past, the shimmering carpet of leaves above the plantation floor were only moments away from admitting the shafts of warming sunlight. The empty buildings and bunkers scattered among the rubber trees along the perimeter road seemed like a city park without people. Stillness reigned as the trucks came to a halt and Noyes and the others clambered down. 'We had come to the right place; the bunker line was empty, except for corpses.'

The dormant scene was revived by our wanderings and energized by the fresh rays of sun. 'The dead watched with dust-covered, void stares. They'd fallen along their pathway through the wire. They'd died in the open roadway and they lay in shattered pieces in the bunkers. Their stories intrigued us. Several of us gathered around a sapper who had died at the entrance to the second abandoned bunker. We stood looking at him and talking about him, his age, and about the cowardly bunker guards. We were joined by two strangers, apparently from a bunker further up the line. No greetings had been exchanged when "The Frog," our youngest and most recent member, wondered what the sapper might hide beneath him. The Frog's foot moved to probe the body, too heavy to flip. One of the strangers exploded with indignation,' Bill Noyes remembers.

'In an instant the man was moving in defense of the dead flesh and we, our tempers flaring, to defend The Frog. The stranger was breathing smoke and fire; we were ready to jump and kill. The second stranger pushed the distraught man back from danger. Unnerved, we unchambered our weapons as the two men walked away. Slowly we settled down to our task of guarding the dead. They lay still and undisturbed until after we had left later on this bright morning.'

Dau Tieng 3rd Brigade Base Camp was attacked on 23 and 24 February 1969. Approximately two or three sapper companies were involved in successfully penetrating the base, a relatively small force. Had the enemy been able to commit a much larger force, a significant victory could possibly have been theirs. Instead, they lost the battle but won the war.

Above: **A recruit clutches his M16 in Vinh Thanh Valley, in May of 1966.** *At right:* **Second Lieutenant George Markadell and men during Operation Masher, in February of 1966.** *Above opposite:* **Men and personnel carriers attack through barbed wire-strewn fields at Long Binh on 31 January 1968.**

These pages: Long Khanh Province, 1966. In the smoke of a battleground yet still smoldering, Sp4 Ruediger Richter lifts his weary eyes to heaven as if in supplication for his fallen comrade-in-arms. Staring meditatively down at the body, Sergeant Daniel Spencer likewise addresses a deeper meaning. These men—GIs of the 4th Battalion, 503rd Infantry, 173rd Airborne Brigade—are foot soldiers as were the men of Troy, or the Roman Legionnaires, but their war is a war in which the commander no longer enters battle with his men, and in which the death-dealing 'spear' is triggered, or launched, or dropped upon them from thousands of feet, or tens of miles away.

When he confronts the enemy, today's soldier faces, and is himself armed with, sophisticated weaponry that is capable of providing the firepower of 10 soldiers of pre-twentieth century history. Even so, there are still the common elements of soldiering—things that every soldier of every age has known: fear, and anger and courage and death. Also, as in World War I's famous Christmas celebration of 1914—an impromptu celebration in 'no man's land,' between the grimy, death-filled trenches, that momentarily made brothers of Allied and Axis troops—there is the possibility of faith, and compassion for the common state of mankind.

Shortly, the men in this photo will hear the *thwack-thwack-thwack* of a helicopter's rotor, and soon after that, a 'Huey' will land briefly, to evacuate their dead buddy from the battle zone.

At top, above: A US Navy Sea, Air and Land (SEAL) team checks their weapons in preparation for a landing from their craft, somewhere on a river in Viet Nam, in October, 1968. *Above:* The same SEAL team scrutinizes the shoreline. *At right:* A SEAL ashore, armed with grenades and an automatic weapon.

At left: SEALs with captured Viet Cong equipment after destroying 'VC' base camps along the Bajjac River during Operation Crimson Tide in September, 1967. *Above:* SEALs on mission in the Rung Sat Special Zone on 13 January 1967. (Photo by Ph1 LR Robinson, US Navy.) *Below:* ARVN Seventh division casualties are readied for evacuation, after heavy combat along the Kinh Xang Canal on 19 January 1963. At the time, the US was covertly involved. (Photo by Pfc Ned Crawley, US Army.)

That fabled tactical construction crew, the US Army Corps of Engineers was vital to the American effort in Vietnam. *Above:* An 'engineer' heads for a construction site in a bulldozer affectionately named for his girlfriend. *Below:* An armored unit helps to get an Army engineers tractor trailer—which itself is transporting another truck—out of the mud. *Above right:* Engineers with a payloader on a tractor trailer. *Below right:* The preparation of a strategic road. (All photos by Jack Casper via Bill Noyes.)

Part of the extensive Mekong Delta is seen in the aerial view *below*. (Photo by M Heacox via Bill Noyes.) *Above:* An American flotilla somewhere in the Mekong Delta. Monitor boats like the one *at left* were known as 'Zippos' (after the famous cigarette lighter company) for their flame-throwing capability. (Photo by George Jokolai.) *At right:* A Strike Assault Boat (STAB) on a high-speed patrol along the Mekong River near the Cambodian border in June, 1970. (Photo by L Bernard Moran, US Navy.)

Civilian relations in South Viet Nam. *At top, above:* Vietnamese peasants are hailed to shore by American GIs. It was precautionally wise to establish the identity of sizable groups of unknown adults in battle-conscious Vietnam. (Photo by Rob Jenkins via Bill Noyes.) *Above:* A Vietnamese boy playing in a water-lily pond. Despite the hostilities, the Vietnamese people went about their normal lives as well as they could. (Photo by M Heacox via Bill Noyes.) *At left:* South Vietnamese Army personnel and refugees from North Vietnam at Xam Moi on 26 March 1968. The flag shown was made by the refugees, and it symbolically depicts the refugees' solidarity with the armed forces of South Vietnam. Personnel of the 11th Vietnamese Airborne Battalion gave the people food, clothing and medical care. (Photo by Sp5 Dallas J Riddle, US Army.)

Above: A 1968 fish-eye lens photo of bombs released by a US Air Force F-105 Thunderchief (colloquially, a 'Thud') over a North Vietnamese target. *At right:* F-105 pilot Colonel AJ Bowman at Tan Son Nhut Air Base, in 1966.

These pages: A view of an Armored unit compound: trucks, personnel carriers and M48 medium tanks are plentifully in evidence. Russ Gamble, who took this photograph, was an advisor with a volunteer unit from Thailand in 1969. Thailand, South Korea, the Philippines, Australia and New Zealand were the nations that joined the US and South Vietnam in the war effort. The US M48 medium tank proved itself the equal of the larger Soviet T54 tank used by North Vietnamese troops. (Photo by Russ Gamble via Bill Noyes.)

TWO DAYS IN JUNE WITH B COMPANY

By Gary P Williams

On 7 June 1968 B Company Second Battalion 60th Infantry Air assaulted an enemy stronghold somewhere near the Plain of Reeds. I was with a small element of Fourth Platoon. At one time we had been a mortar platoon, but now we were just a line platoon.

Were walking along abreast with Second Platoon when the Viet Cong opened up on us and pinned the two platoons down in an open rice paddy. We had to low crawl back to the dike and lay behind it. I recall we had a few guys wounded, as I remember seeing a Second Platoon medic attending them behind a paddy dike, but I do not know why my friend and myself were not hit. We got behind the dike to return incoming small arms fire, firing for the first time ever in combat—two M72 (LAW) rounds at bunkers in a dike 50 yards ahead, where the enemy fire was coming from.

Eventually, we assaulted the bunker line that 'Charlie' had left. We then moved over to where our CO and some other platoon members were moving forward and taking

Above: **Sp4 Danny Hughes sets a trip flare outside Company A's night camp perimeter.** *At right:* **The crew of an M113 armored personnel carrier from the 11th Armored Cavalry idles their vehicle during a pause in a firefight at Long Binh on 23 February 1969. (Photo by Sp4 KL Dowell, US Army.)**

fire from an overgrown area near some nippa palms. Just then, a combat photographer, who had been assigned to our unit for that day, was wounded in the left hand, and the CO yelled and motioned for someone to help him out, so I went to his aid, put a dressing on his hand and evacuated him to the rear of the line. Then he was put on a medevac helicopter. I tried to get his M16 from him, but he wouldn't give it up. (It was our company policy to keep weapons with the unit. You never knew if you would need them.)

When I returned to the main body of company, they were still fighting. Another soldier from the 1st Platoon was wounded when an AK-47 round hit the flash suppresser on his M16, embedding pieces of weapon in his face, temporarily blinding him. I helped him back to the rear of the battlefield and had him dusted off with the help of the battalion sergeant major. Finally, the fighting died down, and the company set up its defensive perimeter for the night. I shared a position with the same friend with whom I'd been pinned down earlier in the day.

In the middle of the night I heard moaning noises coming from one of the bunkers we had cleared during the day. A sergeant from 1st Platoon said he would fire a white star cluster for me if I would crawl from my position to the bunker outside the perimeter and put a grenade in it. Because I was very close to the bunker when the frag grenade exploded, I was hit with a terrific blow in the lower back, which knocked the wind out of me. I thought for a minute I had been hit by shrapnel from the grenade or a secondary explosion from the bunker, but I crawled back to our position in the line and waited the night out.

At left: **Soldiers identified as 'Sergeant Roehm and his company radioman' work out map coordinates, to call in an artillery strike.** *Above:* **His uniform smeared with the grime of combat, an American GI awaits what comes next.**

In the morning, I learned that what hit me must have been a large dirt clod from the bunker or a piece of wood.

We found a mangled VC in the bunker that morning, but couldn't find a weapon. The CO came over to the bunker and congratulated me, as 'body count' was our *numero uno* objective. He asked me if this had been my first confirmed kill, and I told him it was. My main motivation in the kill was revenge for the death of my best friend, who had been killed during the Tet Offensive while fighting at Ben Tre City on 2 February 1968. Even though I had been in country since August 1967, I had a numb feeling.

The next day we were returned to our base camp at Tan Tru.

At left: Marines of D Company in the city of Hue, on 24 February 1968, during the Tet Offensive. *Above:* GIs of the 25th Infantry at Anh Khe stand guard as a Ch-47 Chinook touches down, during Operation Thayer II in January of 1967. (Photo by Pfc John Walker, US Army.) *At top, above:* A First Lieutenant and a radioman of the Fourth Infantry, during Operation Junction City, in March, 1967. (Photo by Pfc James Fitzpatrick, US Army.)

War on the edge of Saigon. *At left:* US Marines conduct a house-by-house search for Viet Cong snipers at Bien Hoa, on 2 February 1968. *Below:* With an armored personnel carrier providing cover, American soldiers make double-time along a landing zone, during a North Vietnamese attack on Bien Hoa, on 26 February 1969. *Above:* While it looks like an automobile scrapyard, this is a city street in the Saigon area, sometime in the late 1960s: note the bullet holes. (Photo by Doug DeLay via Bill Noyes.)

BOOBY TRAP

At approximately 1730 hours, 14 January 1966, the 26-year- old woman shown, and identified, entered the village Committee Office in Tan Thuan Dong hamlet, Cia Dinh Military Sector, (Coordinates XS 896 885 on 1:50,000 AMS Series L701), under the pretense of wanting to apply for a new Identification Card. When asked to wait, she sat down on a wooden bench occupied by three or four other Vietnamese Nationals and placed a paper bag under the bench. (This paper bag contained the timing device and C-2 plastic explosive shown here.) In a few minutes she got up and left the office. A short time later the bag was noticed by other occupants of the office, who opened it and discovered the bomb. They immediately called the National Police, who in turn notified the Military. Source does not know whether the bomb's timing device was faulty or disarmed by the Police and Military. Wondering why the bomb had failed to go off, the woman returned to the vicinity of the office, and was promptly recognized and arrested.

During the course of the preliminary interrogation, the woman stated, 'Don't bother asking me questions, just go ahead and kill me.' She then refused to make any further statements.

The woman was further interrogated throughout the course of the night, at one time being subjected to the 'Water Treatment.' During this period she made the further statement that her reason for planting the bomb in the government office was 'revenge,' as her husband had been killed in a bombing by government planes. The ARVN interrogators feel that this is not true, but rather that the woman is a well-trained Viet Cong 'Agent.'

The timer for the bomb was a CYTAS wrist watch with a small hole drilled through the crystal, at the 12 position, to accommodate the end of an electrical wire. A second wire was attached to the watch case through one of the band pin holes. The hour and sweep second hand had been cut off. The original amount of C-2 plastic explosive used in the construction of the bomb could not be accurately determined, as several parties had taken some prior to it's arrival in Sources' hands. The total amount has been estimated at 2.5 pounds, however.

Any further information on this woman, or incident, will be forwarded.

Photography: Narrative:
James L Kidd   *RV Sutherland*

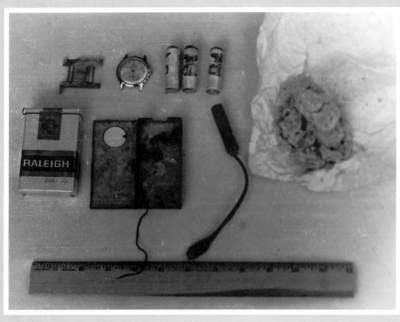

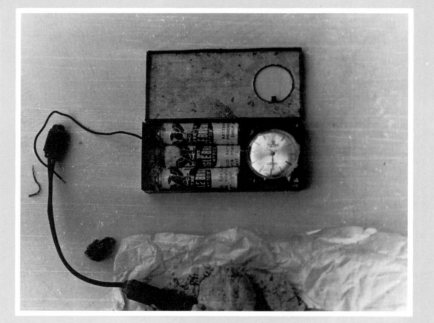

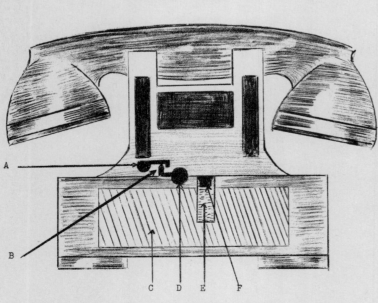

TELEPHONE BOOBYTRAP

Above and above left: **The booby trap described in the text above.** *At right:* **The woman who made and placed the booby trap. The depraved ingenuity with which booby traps are made encompasses a wide range of designs involving innocent-seeming everyday objects. As is discussed *below*, a telephone can be modified to become such an instrument of immediate death. Besides this, transistor radios, tobacco pipes, cigarette packs, flashlights, fountain pens and even so small an object as a police whistle have often been modified to cause serious injury to the unwary user.**

As if that weren't bad enough, there are booby traps within booby traps— you find out the obvious one, and in dismantling it, touch off another that was designed especially to terminate just such a 'smart guy' as you. There are 'whatzis' (phonemic for 'What's this?') booby traps that such feature odd, Rube Goldberg-like objects as hand-crank pulley-operated wall fans loaded with explosives that are meant to excite your curiosity, and when you attempt to 'find out how that thing works'… well, 'curiosity killed the cat.' There are, of course, booby traps like land mines, trip wire-operated explosive charges and/or firearms, gate bombs, door bombs, window bombs—even water canteen bombs and, more sadly still, soda pop and candy bar bombs.

A.— Release Hook   C.— Charge   E.— Detonator
b.— Striker   D.— Spring   F.— Blasting Cap

A **telephone** has been used as boobytrap bait. This illustrates how a simple instrument may be boobytrapped so that detection is most difficult. This is also an illustration of complicated and time-consuming design that could be fashioned only when ample time and special equipment are available. IS YOUR OFFICE, COMMAND POST, CONFERENCE ROOM SECURE? DO YOU REQUIRE IDENTIFICATION BEFORE ALLOWING A TELEPHONE REPAIRMAN TO REPAIR YOUR TELEPHONES?

MICHAEL WITTMUSS: COMBAT CASUALTY

by Michael Wittmuss

During my seven months in the field with Charlie Company, I experienced first hand the medical evacuation system in Vietnam, as I was medevaced by helicopter twice—once for combat wounds and the second time for FUO (fever of unknown origin). I can't say enough in respect to those Marine helicopter crews that came in to extract the wounded, often braving intense enemy ground fire in the process.

By the time I got to Vietnam in late 1968, the medical evacuation and treatment system had been refined to a high art. Eighty-two percent of all seriously wounded Americans were saved by rapid helicopter evacuation to a medical treatment facility. This compares to 71 percent in World War II and 74 percent in Korea. The down side of this was that there were over 10,000 amputees that came out of Vietnam—more than the maimed casualty count of World War II and Korea combined. Ironically, an American soldier wounded in Vietnam stood a better chance of surviving than if he had been injured in a major auto

accident in the United States, as civilian life-flight helicopters were not widely used until the late 1970s.

I was wounded about 10:50 am on the 24th of January 1969—only three days before my 22nd birthday—in Quang Nam province in South Vietnam. Our company, Charlie 1/5, had been out beating the bushes in the Arizona Valley (a rice farming area near An Hoa), looking for the elusive Victor Charlie. After spending about four weeks of splashing through rice paddies and humping up and down mountains, our company was pulled out of the field and sent to a small fortified hilltop encampment near An Hoa for a 'rest.'

For the most part, life in this camp was considered 'skate duty,' or easy duty. Instead of sleeping in an open hole in the ground in the heat, rain and mud like we did out in the bush, we now had tents to sleep in. This camp also had a mess tent that served one hot meal a day. However, there was a down side to this 'easy duty.' A convoy road, which ran from the An Hoa combat base north to Liberty Bridge and then on to Da Nang, passed right by our little hilltop camp.

So every morning while we were in this camp our company had to send a platoon down to the road to provide security for the mine sweeping/clearing teams that checked it for mines and booby traps. Since this duty was rotated among the three platoons in our company, every third day I would have to go out on a mine sweeping operation.

We would leave camp just as the sun was coming up and join the Marine engineers on the road. Sometimes they would bring a little added firepower along with them in the form of a tank or a couple of Amtracks. Our platoon would then divide into squads, with one squad on each side of the road as flank security. We grunts would have to go out about 100 meters into the brush and rice paddies

Above: **A 'tunnel rat' comes back from a subterranean search-and-destroy mission in 1967.** *Below:* **Troopers of the First Cavalry search a village in a joint effort with the South Vietnamese National Police, in Bong Son, in 1967.** *At right:* **Men of the Seventh Marines search a paddy for Viet Cong.**

and move 'on line' with the sweep teams—which were actually a couple of Marine engineers carrying mine detectors that looked like large versions of present-day civilian 'metal detectors.'

The gooks weren't stupid. They planted their mines and booby traps out in the brush far enough away from the road so that grunts walking flank security couldn't see them until they stepped on one. The enemy would also plant a few mines in the road just to keep us guessing.

It seemed like every time we went out we lost someone to a mine or booby trap. We would hear a loud WHAM! out in the fields, then see a column of dirt and smoke fly into the air—or a geyser of water, if the grunt had been walking through a rice paddy. Then there would be cries of 'CORPSMAN! CORPSMAN UP!' I would grab my medical gear and start running, wondering who in our platoon had gotten it this time. The injured Marine would be lucky if he just had a couple of shrapnel wounds. Sometimes he would have lost a foot or a leg.

On this one particular day we had almost completed sweeping our section of the road. I could see the other sweep team coming down the road towards us from the direction of Liberty Bridge. I didn't hear an explosion, but I saw a small cloud of black smoke shoot up into the air about fifty meters away in some heavy scrub brush off to the right side of the road. No one seemed much interested in this, so at first I thought that the other sweep team had located a mine and had blown it in place.

A couple minutes later the Marines up ahead began calling 'CORPSMAN! CORPSMAN UP!' I clutched my medical gear and dashed up the road to where several men were standing in waist high brush in an old abandoned rice paddy. They pointed to where a haze of dark

Above: **Camouflage in Vietnam, 1967.** *At right:* **An M48 tank and two M113 personnel carriers slog through a Vietnamese marsh in August, 1968.**

smoke still hung in the air. I left the road and slowly and carefully made my way through the tall brush. I remember that one Marine shouted at me, 'Watch your step, doc! I think this whole damn field is full of booby traps!'

I found three wounded Marines sprawled in the brush. I could still smell the pungent odor of burnt gunpowder all around us. One of the Marines had tripped a booby trap mine.

Quickly, I looked over the three men. They appeared to have shrapnel wounds in their legs. I picked the guy who seemed to be in the worst shape and went to work on him. There was already a large pool of congealing blood under his right leg. I slit open his pants leg with my knife to expose his leg. It had been badly chewed up by shrapnel and was hemorrhaging. I began putting on pressure dressings to control the bleeding. By this time several Marines had arrived and were trying to comfort the other two injured men. One asked, 'What can we do to help you, doc?'

I threw him a bandoleer of my battle dressings and told him to 'patch up any bleeding holes you find on those two!'

The other two casualties seemed to be doing all right — at least they were conscious and able to talk. One man was even sitting up, his bloody legs stretched out in front of him as he watched with interest as a fellow Marine applied battle dressings.

The guy I was working on wasn't doing as well. He was unconscious. I felt his pulse and checked him over closely. His skin was turning an ashen-gray color. 'Shit!' I thought. 'He's going into shock.'

At left: **Outgoing mail, 1968: Sergeant Gerald Benzel of the 101st Airborne collects 'those important letters home' from his men during a landing zone clearing in the A Shau Valley. (Photo by Sp4 Vaughn Reichelderfer, US Army.)**
Above: **Major Ben Crosby of the 25th Infantry discovers the breathing tubes of a Viet Cong underground hideout, north of Duc Pho in 1967.**

Luckily, a corpsman from the other sweep team came running up with a bottle of an intravenous blood volume expander solution. I managed to get a needle into the unconscious man's vein and began pumping the fluid into his body. I examined his body for additional wounds and then rechecked his pulse. His pulse felt stronger and his skin color start to come back.

A Marine with a radio on his back appeared. 'Doc,' he said, 'I have a medevac chopper on the way to our position. They want to know what the situation is here.'

'Tell them I have three casualties. Frag wounds, lower extremities. One emergency, two priority.'

About 10 minutes later I heard the WHOP WHOP WHOP sound of rotor blades as a helicopter circled high overhead. It was one of those Marine CH-46s, a monstrous, tandem-rotored machine. It spiraled down out of the sky and landed a dozen yards in front of us, its rotor blades lashing us with flying dust and debris. We carried the wounded on board the chopper and watched it lift off. Then I turned and start to walk back to collect my medical gear.

That's when someone tripped another booby trap mine! I don't remember hearing the sound of an blast, but I seem to recall seeing clods of earth whiz by my face. Then a black curtain seemed to pass across my mind.

Above: **A CH-46 Sea Knight—US Marine counterpart to the US Army Chinook. (Photo by Gary Wittmuss.)** *Below:* **A Fifth Royal Australian Regiment GI, with Australian F1 rifle and an anti-tank weapon, in 1969.** *At right:* **A 25th Infantry joint mission with Vietnamese Popular Forces. (Photo by Sp5 RC Lafoon, US Army.)**

I guess the blast from the explosion knocked me down and I blanked out for several seconds.

The first thing I remember when my mind cleared was wondering, 'What the hell am I doing on the ground?' There was a Marine bending over me with a worried look on his face. He seemed to be talking to me, but I couldn't hear him because my ears were ringing.

The rest of what happened that day was just like watching one of those old, silent movies—one that had been badly spliced together. I only recall jumbled 'scenes' of what took place. I remember staggering about in a confused state for a few minutes and seeing three or four Marines lying on the ground and several more stumbling around, all covered with blood. The radioman, who was sitting down, clutched his bloody stomach with one hand as he talked into his radio, trying to contact the medevac chopper that had just taken off so he could bring it back. I bent over a Marine lying on the ground. He looked up at me and said something, but I still couldn't hear anything. His pants were ripped open and there was a huge gash on his inner thigh, and a small fountain of blood was gushing out of the wound. I pulled a battle dressing out of one of my pockets and thrust it into the wound. I put another dressing on top of that one and tied it down tight to make a pressure dressing.

Some time later a helicopter landed nearby. The crewmen jumped out and help to load the casualties. A Marine standing next to me pointed to my right arm. There was a trickle of blood running down the length of my arm. I rotated my arm and saw a small hole near the elbow from which blood was squirting out.

'Oh!' I thought. 'I'm wounded.' My arm didn't hurt, it just felt sort of numb. I handed the Marine a battle dressing and he applied it to my arm.

After we boarded the medevac helicopter, I crouched on the floor next to a man whose face was covered with several bloody bandages. He was waving one of his arms about. I grabbed his hand and squeezed it. That seemed to calm him down.

The chopper was packed with over half a dozen wounded men, and the ride probably took at least twenty

Above: **A muddy 60th Infantry GI after a rice paddy firefight in 1969.** *At right:* **Is the smoke from a marker or a mine? Three GIs in the dangerously concealing Buffalo grass await an incoming 'Huey.'** (Photo by George Jokolai.)

minutes, but to me it seemed that we had just taken off and then we were landing again.

The helicopter landed at the 95th Army Surgical Hospital near Da Nang, next to a large quonset hut type building. The building was a triage area, where casualties were sorted and evaluated as to their type of wounds and treatment required. Half a dozen medics came sprinting out of the building carrying litters to unload the helicopter. I walked in the building, and a medic asked me if I was wounded. I pointed to the dressing on my arm, and he told me to lie down on a nearby stretcher.

Although this place appeared to be in total confusion, it was actually very organized, as Army medics and doctors rushed about tending to the incoming casualties. As I lay there, I could hear helicopters landing and taking off outside as more casualties were brought in.

The medics brought in a stretcher with a guy on it and laid him down just a few feet from me. One side of his head was wrapped with several large, bloody battle dressings. A doctor and several medics hurried over to check him out.

'Hey!' the doctor shouted. 'This guy is dead. Get this body out of here!'

I glanced over at the stretcher. The medics had removed the dressings and exposed a hole in the side of his head you could have shoved your fist into. Bits of brain matter and blood were dripping out of the wound. 'Jeeze!' I thought to myself, and turned away.

An Army medic came over to me, removed the combat equipment I was still wearing, and began cutting off all my clothes. Pretty soon I was completely naked. He took my blood pressure on one arm and then stuck a needle in my other arm and hooked me up to a bottle of intravenous

Above: **US Air Force combat controller Sergeant William York, at Tan Son Nhut Air Base in 1968.** *At top, above:* **GIs use a chemical personnel detector in 1967.** *At left:* **A Huey and equipment for Operation Somerset Plain.**

fluid. He cut the dressing from my arm and put a gauze pad over the wound.

After he was finished, a female Army nurse came over to me and began asking me questions as to my name, rank, unit, etc. The ringing in my ears had stopped so I could hear what she was saying. I'm sure I must have blushed a deep red because I didn't have a stitch of clothes on, but she didn't seem to notice.

Then a doctor examined my wound, redressed it and told the medics to take me to Radiology. The medics threw a blanket over me and wheeled me away. As we passed through the door, I looked back into the room. It was jammed with bloody men on stretchers. The floor was littered with discarded battle dressings and pools of half-dried blood.

'Shit! What a frigging butcher shop this place is!' I thought.

In Radiology they took an X-ray of my arm. A few minutes later I was on a hospital ward in a bed with clean, white sheets. I guess the shock was wearing off because my arm began to throb with pain. An Army nurse came up to my bed and asked if I wanted a shot for the pain. 'Hell, yes!' I told her.

After receiving the pain medication, I quickly fell asleep. I slept all day and night and didn't wake up until the next morning. Doctors, nurses and medics came around later in the morning on doctor's rounds to evaluate each patient and discuss treatment.

Later, a doctor pulling a metal treatment stand came over to my bed. He introduced himself and told me that he was going to remove that piece of metal that was in my arm. He disposed of the dressing and cleaned the wound with surgical soap. Then he put on a pair of sterile gloves and placed a sterile towel over my arm. He jabbed the needle of a syringe into my arm and told me that it was a local anesthetic that might burn a little. It sure did! The fluid felt like fire going into my arm!

Immediately my arm began to grow pleasantly numb. The doctor stripped off his gloves and checked my X-ray. I told him that I was a Navy corpsman, a medic, and I would like to see the X-ray, if I could.

'Sure,' he said, and handed it to me.

It was a radiograph of my elbow joint. A shard of metal, about the size of my thumb, was in the muscle near the elbow joint. The doctor said I was lucky; had the fragment gone in deeper, it would have severed a major nerve in my arm. I noted a number of small specks on the X-ray, like grains of sand, sprinkled along the length of my arm and asked him about them. He said they were probably bits of metal, sand or dirt that had been driven into my arm by the force of the explosion. They were too small and numerous to extract, but they shouldn't bother me—they might stay in my arm forever, or eventually work themselves out to the surface.

He put on another pair of sterile gloves and went to work on my arm with a scalpel and a pair of tweezers. I could vaguely feel him digging around in my arm for several minutes, and then he held up a small, jagged fragment and wanted to know if I wanted to keep it as a souvenir.

'Hell, no!' I said.

After suturing the wound closed and putting a clean dressing over it, he told me I would be staying at this hospital for several days, and then I would be sent to a convalescent center for a few weeks. The IV would also stay hooked to my arm for another day as they planned to give me a powerful antibiotic. I was relieved to hear that I wasn't going to be sent right back into the field again.

I checked out my surroundings. There were about 30 patients on the ward. A few of them were Marines, but

At right: **Army of the Republic of South Vietnam First Division troops board Hueys in the A Shau Valley during Operation Somerset Plain in 1968. The troops are dropped off in a battle zone, and the helicopters pick up casualties for the return trip. (Photo by Sp4 Vaughn Reichelderfer, US Army.)**

most of them were Doggies (soldiers). Then I noticed a foul odor. I lifted my blanket and realized the bad smell was me! I hadn't had a real bath in weeks—unless you call wading across a few chest-deep rivers having a bath. Since I was ambulatory, I asked a nurse for some soap, a hospital robe and plastic to wrap around my dressing. After hanging my IV bottle on a long pole with little wheels on the bottom (called an IV stand), my pole and I went off to take a shower. The shower made me feel like a million bucks! How good it felt to get the stink of Vietnam off my body.

I was watching the patients on my ward come and go and thought to myself, 'You lucky stiff! Here are all these guys messed up in a hundred different ways and all you have is a little arm wound.' Then I realized that I still had more than nine months to go in Vietnam. Shoot! It was very possible that I could be wounded again! I tried not to think about it; it was too depressing.

That evening I heard that a movie would be shown on another ward, so my IV stand and I went off to watch a movie. The movie screen was a large, white sheet tacked to a wall. Of all the movies they could have shown, they chose to show us a John Wayne film called *The Green Berets*—a Vietnam war movie! I like John Wayne, but I thought this movie was a load of crap. An over-aged and overweight actor tramping through the jungle in clean and neatly pressed jungle camies while mowing down hordes of nasty commies had nothing to do with the reality of the war that I was involved in! Most of the patients laughed and hooted at the movie and, like me, left before it was over.

The next day I was off the ward for a while. When I returned there was a small black box and a piece of paper on my bed. I opened the lid on the box and inside was a large, heart-shaped, gold and purple-colored medallion attached to a purple ribbon. The paper was a certificate from the President of the United States stating that I had been awarded the Purple Heart for 'Wounds Received In Action.'

'So that's what a Purple Heart looks like,' I thought. It was a nice looking medal.

'Hey, doc!' one of the patients yelled at me. 'You missed the show! Some Army brass were just here passing out the Purple Hearts to the wounded. They had a photographer with them—you could have gotten your picture taken with some Army brass.'

'I'm Navy,' I told him. 'Why would I want a mug shot taken with your Doggie officers?'

At left: **The troops and supplies have been unloaded from the US Army CH-47 Chinook transport, and the job of digging in on a Vietnamese hilltop must begin.** *Above:* **An alert and wary US Marine in a combat construction zone.**

I looked at the certificate again. Some Army clerk had typed in the incorrect designation for my Navy rate and rank.

'Oh, well,' I thought. 'What does an Army clerk know about the Navy? I'll get it changed later.' I mailed the medal home to my folks for safekeeping.

The following day I was loaded aboard an Air Force ambulance plane and flown further down south. We landed on an airfield somewhere near the Cam Rahn Bay Naval Base, where all of us new arrivals were put on several Army ambulance buses and taken to the Sixth Army Convalescent Center. The center was located on a beach facing the South China Sea. As I remember, the place was hot as hell!

The beach was made of clean, white sand. At midday you couldn't walk across it with bare feet, it was so hot. However, you couldn't go swimming in the ocean. There was barbed wire strung out in the water and they had anti-personnel mines buried along the shoreline. I guess that was to keep the enemy out, and us in!

I was assigned to a ward hut—a long, wooden building containing about 30 patients. We all slept on Army cots. The building was not air conditioned. The Army medical officer in charge of our ward was short handed and needed help. When he found out that I was a Navy medic, he placed me and another Navy corpsman in charge of patient care for our ward. It was a pretty easy job. Most of our patients were Army guys whose wounds were almost completely healed. I just had to give out medications, administer injections and dress wounds.

My convalescence was a lot better than what most of the patients there had to go through. Every day they had to muster for 'Rehabilitation Physical Fitness Training,' which consisted mostly of filling countless sandbags in the blazing sun for several hours each day.

I stayed at the center for about three weeks. I received my release orders the last week of February 1969 and was flown up north to Qui Hjon, then to Chu Lai and on to Da Nang. I hitched a helicopter ride from Da Nang to the An Hoa Combat Base, and a few short days later I was back in the dirt and mud with Charlie Company.

Above: **Grenade launcher propped across his knee, Pfc George Nagel uses a sewing machine found in a Viet Cong tunnel, in 1967.** *At right:* **A platoon sergeant takes a break, with his M16 close at hand. (Photo by George Jokolai.)**

At top, above: A camouflaged ARVN sniper takes aim with a vintage M1 Garand. *Above:* US advisors take lunch with Vietnamese battalion commanders during a search-and-destroy operation in 1965. It was still a time of some optimism for the war-weary South Vietnamese: the US was just beginning to openly exercise its might on their behalf. *At right:* Two South Vietnamese Special Forces rangers return to the Fifth Special Forces camp after heavy action on patrol. The M1s they carry mark an early stage of US involvement, when the handier M16 was not yet availed to Vietnamese troops.

Letter found on the body of an NVA Regular after the Tet Offensive 40 miles northwest of Saigon

5 March 1968

My dearest love,

I received another letter from you the day before yesterday, 3 March. In your letter you said that you haven't received any mail from me, even the one I sent on 17 February. Therefore, I had to write this letter immediately, otherwise you will wait too long.

My love, so you are going out to the battlefield, aren't you? Last Sunday, when coming back home, Miss Tuyet told me that you were about to go on operation pretty soon; but in your previous letter, you still didn't tell me anything about it.

If you have to leave, I would like you not to worry about anything, even about me. You should think of nothing else but your duty, and try to achieve victory so that the day when you return, we can be happy together. We are now so far away from each other, and I don't know when we can see each other again.

As for me, everything is going as usual. I haven't had any days off since Tet (New Year Festival), and it was not until last Sunday that I was allowed to come home for a visit. But as soon as I got home, I had a real bad time with my mother. She blamed and scorned me the minute she saw me on the porch. Someone had said that your parents already made the proposal of our marriage and something else I don't know, but mom got upset.

My dearest love, whenever I came home and was scorned like that, I always thought about it for days, and was very sad. As to you, I understand you more and more, and love you very much, but I don't know whether we will be able to see each other again or not. At the present time, my love, please forget everything I have just said. We will wait until the day of victory, when you come back, then we will talk about it.

My dearest love, last Sunday when I visited your parents, they gave me your diary, which you had asked them to. Your father also told me that you were sick and looked very thin when he went to visit you the other day. I am so sad and worry very much to hear that you still have to go out fighting a battle while you are sick like that. I know that you are now at a place which is very, very far from here, but I cannot imagine where it is. My love, please take good care of yourself and recover soon so that you won't be behind your friends in your duty. As for me, I was also sick the other day and had to stay in bed for two days, but now I am fine.

My dearest love, please don't think about what I have said and don't be sad. You wrote in your diary that you are afraid that I will be sad when reading the diary. I must confess that I was a little bit sad at first; but it was all my fault, I didn't have a chance to talk with you more so that you can understand me.

Now that I have known you more, I promise that I won't be sad, and my love, promise me that you won't think about it any more either.

I have to stop here. May God bring you good health and happiness.

Your love,

I hope to see you as soon as possible.

Although it was war, life went on. Love, as witnessed by the text on this page, and work, as witnessed by the photo *at left*—of rubber workers at the Cau Khoi Plantation in 1969—continued despite the hostilities. (Photo by Bill Noyes.)

Above: Fairchild C-123Bs of the 12th Air Commando Squadron fly a defoliation mission, to destroy sniper cover and reveal Viet Cong strongholds. Such missions were extremely controversial, as the defoliants used were carcinogenic and caused long-term pollution of watersheds. *Right:* A 19th Tactical Airlift Squadron C-123K transport over Vietnam paddy fields circa 1970. (Photo by S/Sgt Andy Sarakon.)

At left: Marines storm a slope about three miles from the DMZ, in heavy combat with North Vietnamese regulars, during Operation Hastings in July of 1966. *Above:* A Sikorsky CH-54 heavy-lift helicopter airlifts a damaged howitzer from an artillery base.

Below: Cambodia, 1970—chasing the enemy in its sanctuary: Captain Ramon Costa and GIs of the 27th Infantry. Since American forces had long been barred from pursuing the enemy into Cambodia, these later encroachments came as a surprise to some.

Above, at top and at right: CH-46 Sea Knights lift off and land on helicopter carriers anchored near the coast of Vietnam. *Above middle:* Crewmen roll out a US Marine UH-34 Seahorse. The use of helicopters in the Vietnam War allowed an unprecedented versatility in transporting supplies and personnel to theaters of battle. Helicopters also allowed rapid transport of casualties to treatment centers. (Photos by Ken Gilpatrick via Bill Noyes.)

Above: Looking nervous, Viet Cong prisoners await interrogation at a South Vietnamese military installation in the mid-1960s. *At right:* Interrogation of a suspected Viet Cong in 1965. The first questions on the notebook's left page are 'Are there any VC in this village? Are you VC?' *At top, above:* A wary village girl along Highway 14 in 1968. (Photo by Bill Noyes.)

BIDING TIME

When the colors were sent home, those of the Second Battalion of the 27th Marines staying in country were transferred. Navy Corpsman Doug Condit was sent to the Seventh Marine Battalion, which was stationed directly behind Red Beach, near 'beautiful downtown Da Nang.' When he arrived, a 'first-class' (E6) was in charge of the corpsmen at the Seventh Engineers, and Condit was assigned to bunk with 1st Bridge Company. The corpsmen were attached to different areas of the compound, in order that during an attack, all of them would not be maimed at once. Condit was an E5, so he shared a barracks with another E5 corpsman and a Marine sergeant. 'Three of us in a barracks constructed for 30 Marines.' he recalls. 'What luxury!'

Since it was an engineer battalion, there was a sink with hot and cold running water in the barracks, as well as a television set and a stereo, a mess hall table and a round card-playing table. It also had electric lights and a refrigerator. Compared with being with the Second Battalion, it was heaven!

When Condit arrived at Seventh Engineers, the First Class was impressed by the idea of getting a grunt corpsman, so he assigned Condit as the POIC in charge of sick call. The dental clinic was air-conditioned, and the Naval Chaplain—a Southern Baptist minister—regularly hung out there. 'Boy, did he and I have verbal exchanges,' Condit recalls, 'to which he would usually answer, "Well,

Above: **A US soldier meets an Asian elephant. (Photo by Jack Casper via Bill Noyes.)** *Below:* **The Bob Hope Show at the American Amphitheater in Chu Lai, 1969. (Photo by Lou Graul Eisenbrandt.)** *At right:* **American GI Eugene Sissler writes home from Vietnam on Christmas, 1969. (Photo by Bill Noyes.)**

that sounds like an Episcopalian to me." He knew I was Episcopalian.'

The Seventh Engineers spent a warm Christmas with Manhattans and even a cherry. For the Bob Hope show, they were allowed one ticket per corpsman.

'We drew lots,' Doug Condit remembers. 'I lost. But those of us who were not on-call that day were allowed to go to Da Nang to watch the show from the mountain above the amphitheater. They had the outside theatre wired off with mounds of wire—curly barbed wire that the Marines used in combat—and they had Marine MPs every 10 to 15 feet to keep people without tickets from entering the compound. Shortly before the show began, a large group of Marines near me threw their flack jackets on top of the wire and started entering the amphitheater. I had a choice: follow them or get trampled to death (as the MPs had been), so I entered. The show was great. Thanks Bob!'

Around Christmas the Seventh Engineers got an E7 chief who was an alcoholic, but it didn't matter though, because Condit ran the BAS and sick call, and set the watch. Every weekend he would allow the Marines who were off to leave the base for Da Nang, and the rest would hang out on-base at the clubs if they wanted to. Only the duty corpsmen had to stay. 'In all, the BAS was running great,' Condit remembers. 'Then it happened! One day— a Sunday—two chiefs from the Division Surgeon's office showed up in pressed and starched fatigues! (Impressive for a combat zone.)' They were surprised to find only Condit and one other corpsman in the BAS (even the doctor was in town), so they went next door to see the chief, then left in a hurry.

A war of heroism and pathos. *Above:* Sergeant Audrey Crumb, recipient of two silver stars for gallantry in action, and two bronze stars for heroism, takes lunch in Vietnam. (Photo by Bill Noyes.) *At right:* A wounded school girl awaits treatment by an American medic. (Photo by M Heacox via Bill Noyes.)

Condit went next door—it was about 1:30 pm—and the chief was drunk. 'There were numerous open bottles in his hootch, the most prominent being a bottle of Crown Royal. There were also poker chips lying all over the place. The place looked as if it had not been cleaned in *years*. The chief had about a week's growth of beard on his face, and had crumbs and other types of garbage in his beard. He looked like he had urinated on himself. I was in shock.

'I quickly got a hold of as many corpsmen as I could and we quickly made the BAS shine! About 90 minutes later a whole procession of Marine and Navy brass, led by the DiviDoc (ie, Division Surgeon), came marching in. The DiviDoc was a short, boisterous man and, I was told, a gynecologist by trade. Imagine, the Doc in charge of all the medical care of the entire First Marine Division, in combat, in Vietnam was a gynecologist! Needless to say, he tried to show what chaos our BAS was in. I think his men were impressed with the quality, accuracy and up-to-datedness of our medical and personnel records, but the DiviDoc was not impressed with our chief. As the shit was hitting the proverbial fan, I immediately sought out the first sergeant of Headquarters company and arranged to go on R&R to Bangkok two days later, with a sergeant friend of mine from Headquarters company. I believe we bumped a couple of other EMs, but I didn't want to be at the BAS when heads rolled!'

Now that he was a 'short-timer' in Vietnam Doug Condit got to go to Bangkok. 'I don't know if it was due to the political situation at the BAS or just the war, but when our flight was returning to Da Nang, and we got regulation tracers fired at us, I was scared! When I got back to the BAS, my return was eagerly awaited. The Chief had been busted and transferred to First Med Battalion (where I later learned he died of non-combat causes. I've always wondered if he drank himself to death). We had a new Chief and a new first-class, both charged with getting and keeping the place in order. They both came on with that Mr Tough Guy sort of approach.

After I rapped with the two new Mr Tough Guys and showed them what great shape the BAS was—without 'effective' leadership—they backed off! As long as we looked great on paper (which we did) and were providing superb medical care (which we were), they looked great. So the day-to-day running of the BAS really didn't change much. Finally, my relief showed up. I oriented him one week and just hung out as a resource person the next.'

Above: **Children at a relocation camp: war meant displacement for many Vietnamese. (Photo by Doug DeLay via Bill Noyes.)** *At left:* **A USO show in the open air, 'for our boys in Vietnam.' (Photo by Ken Gilpatrick via Bill Noyes.)**

Christmas in Vietnam. *These pages:* A Second Battalion, 27th Infantry 'Wolf-hounds' bunker at the Michelin Rubber Plantation on 25 December 1968. Atop and upon the sandbags is a recoilless rifle, canteens, an M16 and munitions canisters. Though a holiday for westerners, the enemy had no respect for holidays—as was soon evidenced by the Tet Offensive. The decision for 'Vietnamization' had been made, and the long, painful US troop withdrawal would begin in less than a year. (Photo by Bill Noyes.)

BACK TO THE WORLD

The 'whap-whap' sound of approaching chopper blades breaks the heavy silence of a steamy night. A noisy rush of sandy air follows closely behind. Booted footsteps race to waiting litters. The clank of glass bottles filled with life-saving intravenous fluids is echoed above the murmured orders of physicians and the gentle, comforting voices of nurses. Medical personnel in olive-drab fatigues or turquoise scrub suits move in a calm, but lightning-swift pace, for each second is a matter of life or death.
—*Lou Graul Eisenbrandt*

This scenario, familiar for years now to the viewers of the television show 'M*A*S*H,' was a part of Lou Eisenbrandt's daily existence as an emergency room Army nurse in South Vietnam. From the time she arrived at the 91st Evacuation Hospital in Chu Lai in November 1969, until she boarded a C-130 for the flight to Cam Ranh Bay and ultimately back to 'the world' a year later, she was part of the same lifesaving drama that was immortalized in M*A*S*H.

Her first three months at the 91st were spent on a medical ward where GIs were treated for a number of conditions perpetrated by a daily existence in dank forests, polluted river beds and mosquito-infested swamps. Intestinal parasites, malaria, dysentery, hepatitis and jungle rot (caused by wearing rain-soaked boots twenty-four hours a day) could each assure a soldier a warm, dry bed on her ward. Unfortunately, these patients knew that as soon as the doctors and 'angels of mercy' had cured their maladies, they would be back to wading waist-deep in brown water and eyeing each Vietnamese as a potential enemy. It was always difficult to distinguish between the 'good guys' and the 'bad guys.'

After three months on Ward 5, Eisenbrandt was approached by the chief nurse about an opening in the R&E (Receiving and Emergency). 'Trying not to display my hesitation, I accepted,' she recalled. 'My mother had always encouraged her children to look upon new experiences as challenges to be met and "made the most of." Never have I undertaken a greater nursing challenge.'

Her eight and one-half months in the R&E were filled

Above and at right: **US Army 91st Evacuation Squadron nurse Lou Graul Eisenbrandt and pals in Vietnam. (Photos courtesy of Lou Graul Eisenbrandt.)**

with days of three or four grunts wounded by shrapnel in an ambush, interspersed with depressing nights of teen-aged soldiers killed while walking point. She recalls a 15-hour on-duty day when a Vietnamese village was over-run, resulting in 99 casualties, and she can still smile about a night shift of only one patient—with a severely ingrown toenail.

'My memory tries to block out a young man so badly wounded when he stepped on a mine that his legs were missing and his back remained on the litter when we attempted to roll him to one side. My consciousness will never blot out the hurt on the face of an injured child or the words of a fellow nurse: "He may lose both legs," as a friend was wheeled into surgery. Even time will never remove these images so deeply etched into my being.'

It is these poignant memories that have caused some nurses who served in Vietnam to still suffer psychological repercussions—flashbacks, angry outbursts, social dis-trust, alcohol and drug dependency—and difficulties with close personal relationships. For some members of hospital teams, life consisted of work, sleep, a few beers at the officers' club, and free time spent alone in a room, where the destructive images of the war could eat away at even the strongest of souls. Many women, in particular, avoided developing any close friendships with their male coworkers for fear of getting a 'reputation.' Still others

Despite the war, there was sometimes a chance to relax, as is evidenced by trooper Arthur Harp—*at right*, near Tay Ninh in 1968; and *below*, buying a soda near the Ben Cui Plantation in 1969. (Photos by Bill Noyes.) *Opposite:* Cliff Schnack, a CO, on break during Tet, 1969. (Photo by George Jokolai.)

tried to blot out the war in just the opposite fashion, exchanging a few hours of fun for a chance to escape. For Eisenbrandt, neither course seemed a feasible solution.

'My "survival kit" in the Vietnam War arrived at the 91st a few months after I did. As a physician whose specialty dictated working in the emergency room arena, we developed a unique working relationship. Even in tense, crisis situations, we were able to function alongside each other with a quiet understanding of the other person's thoughts and needs. He knew when a smile or anecdote was needed to lighten the too somber mood. I sensed when to ignore a few foul words as he groped to find even one usable vein in a patient in deep shock. It seemed natural that our compatibility would eventually reach beyond the work area.'

It was difficult at an evac hospital to separate work time from off-duty hours. In reality, one was on call at all times. When the sound of dust-off blades became too frequent, one would head to the R&E to see if an extra pair of hands were needed. Therefore, sharing one's free time with someone in the same line of work allowed each to more fully understand when the other was called to help.

'I quickly realized that developing this special friendship helped both of us tolerate the debilitating diseases of war — loneliness, fear, loss of self-worth, anger, paranoia, and boredom brought on by one's daily routine. We looked forward to our free time as a chance to listen to music, share a glass of wine, check out the new merchandise at the PX (usually Beanie-weanies, pants hangers and condoms), or just talk. Our conversations covered many topics, from concern over a gravely wounded patient to the latest truths and fallacies in the *Stars And Stripes*.

'We often shared the happenings of our relatives back home from their recent letters. On some occasions we would muse over how our lives would be different if we'd met in another time and place, but we knew better than to dwell on this for too long. Many evenings saw parties somewhere on the hospital compound and, as nearly everyone knew everyone else, we often joined in the drinking and frivolity. Once again, it helped to forget for a couple of hours that one's family was 19,000 miles away. One could also block out the rumored marches by Americans protesting our participation in the war.

'The positive outcome of our togetherness went far beyond simply facilitating the passage of time. It is said

Above: **US Army doctors operate on a casualty and calm a man in the operating room. (Photo by Lou Graul Eisenbrandt.)** *At right:* **A surgeon in the glare of operating lamps in Vietnam. (Photo by Ken Gilpatrick via Bill Noyes.)**

that the more love one receives, the more, in turn, he or she is able to give. How crucial this giving of love was for a nurse in Vietnam! Each patient, regardless of the severity of his wounds, needed to feel loved, needed to know that someone cared about his survival. On more than one occasion, the bloodied form in torn, green fatigues, lying on the litter, would stare at me through blood-shot, glazed eyes and say, "Hey, you kinda look like my gal back home." What a time to return that love with a squeeze of his hand. Bitterness and anger towards the war had no business here!

'Let me not give the impression, however, that the suffering inflicted on the Americans, as well as on the inhabitants of South Vietnam, did not affect me. Like many who served in the Vietnam War, I deplored the killing, maiming and destruction of another's civilization. And for what prize? Many vets were ostracized, ridiculed and discriminated against upon their return to the States. Was this a fitting welcome home? Verbalizing these frustrations with someone who felt likewise helped heal the psychological wounds before they could fester.

'Who did not wish they could be savoring turkey and cranberries around a white-clothed table at Christmas rather than ingesting powdered eggs and liquid Jello in a steamy, damp mess hall? How could one not feel a surge of anger at being denied the chance to see their newborn child enter the world? How many of us would shed no tears as we licked our birthday cake frosting from a smashed CARE package lid? I wept often; it cleansed my mind. My friend understood, offered a dry shoulder, and never laughed at my puffy, reddened eyes or loud nose-blowing. (I'm not a dainty soap-opera sobber!) When he needed comforting, I responded likewise.

Above: **Christmas cheer, despite the war—cross-bedecked, smiling Sergeant Garza, at the Michelin Rubber Plantation on 25 December 1968. (Photo by Bill Noyes.)** *At right:* **Fire Base 14, a 25th Infantry mortar emplacement near Kon Tum, in April 1968. (Photo by Sp4 Joseph LeBlanc, US Army.)**

'We also shared the joyous times. I've often said of my year in Vietnam, "We worked hard and we played hard." My regular schedule was twelve hours on-duty, six days a week. But we valued our free time and filled many hours with craziness. We water skied in the South China Sea, towed by a boat secured through careful bartering. (We couldn't go out after noon, however; the sharks took over then!) A volleyball net served as a means of aerobic exercise and friendly competition. We lathered on coconut oil to soak up rays on a postage stamp-sized beach at the foot of a cliff. Since I could carry a tune and pluck the guitar, many evenings involved friends, music and free-flowing wine. On rare occasions an available jeep meant a chance to explore life outside the compound. Whether a goodwill visit to the nearby orphanage or a twilight soiree to the Jaded Duck restaurant (remember "Rosie's" in M*A*S*H?) a few miles away, those trips helped relieve that claustrophobic feeling. I relished those opportunities with a close companion.

'From the first moment that Uncle Sam randomly shoved us together, we knew that when our tour of duty ended, so would our relationship. We each had separate lives and circumstances to return to and agreed to not let Vietnam complicate those situations. This decision did not, however, lessen our love for each other, nor did it make that October morning in 1970 any less painful for the two of us.

'As we jostled along the road to a nearby airfield, conversation was nearly absent. Each of us was speculating on what lay ahead for the other. I was relieved to know that my parents could soon worry less as I would be back on friendly ground. I also knew that this goodbye would hurt deeply—he still had five months with the war. I would not be there when his eyes misted, his shoulders ached, or his lips smiled. He, who had been so vital a part of this incredible year of my life, could not be shared with my friends and family. They would hear about helicop-

Above: **A medical corpsman with a Montagnard orphan at the 91st Evacuation Squadron hospital at Chu Lai in February, 1970.** *At right:* **Christmas on Ward 5, in 1969. (Photos by Lou Graul Eisenbrandt.)**

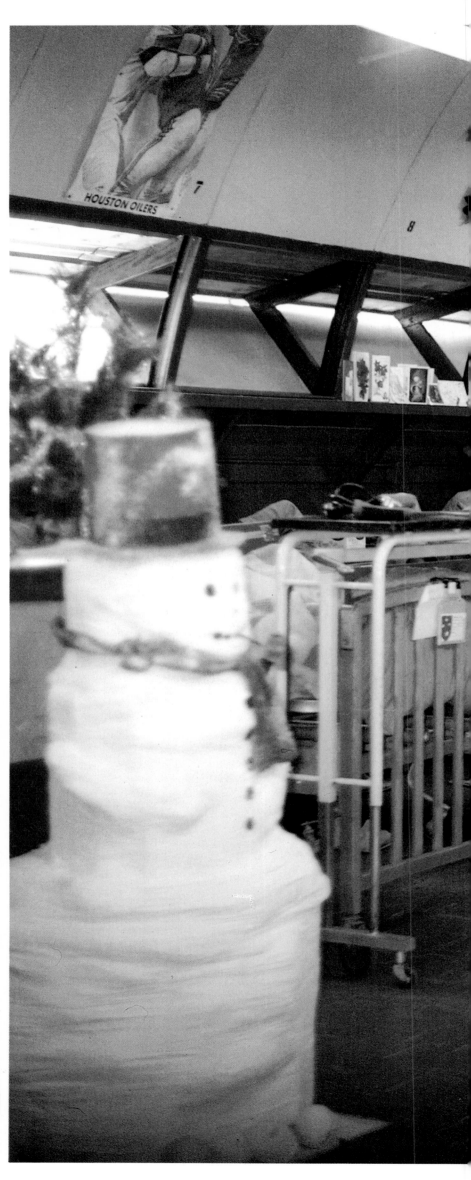

ters, mortar attacks, my work, the patients—but not him. They would not understand.

'Even as I now recall those last moments before I stepped inside the plane, my eyes are damp. We stood in the sweltering heat—me in ill-fitting Class As, he in those familiar fatigues—and held each other until the pain eased. As words brought tears, we said goodbye with our eyes. I boarded the C-130, found a seat and watched until the clouds enveloped my plane. How could I have been so sad on such a happy occasion?

'My return from Southeast Asia was not greeted with boos, demonstrations or hatred from my friends. The residents of my small southern Illinois community looked upon me as they had all other veterans as far back as the Civil War. There was no Main Street parade, just quiet acceptance and prayers of gratitude for my safe return. Aware of the anti-war activities in other parts of the country, I was grateful for their support.

'I found another source of comfort in frequent letters from my special friend still in Chu Lai. As I lost myself within the lines describing an existence I remembered so well, I felt a sense of relief. My adjustment from the war zone to the real world would be a gradual one, not a shock to my system. His letters allowed me to see changes occurring, slowly making the 91st less familiar to me. I responded with words of encouragement and news of mutual friends now enjoying civilian life. Little did we realize at the time how therapeutic those letters were, for both of us.

'While rummaging through an old trunk nearly 20 years later, I found those long-forgotten letters. The last one was dated 26 March—just two weeks before he left for civilization. He often wrote, "We'll meet again; I'm sure of it." Perhaps…

'Over the years I've thought of him from time to time, but only recently have I understood how truly important he was in my life.'

At right: **US Army GIs line up for the National Airlines flight home at Bien Hoa in 1970. (Photo by Sp5 LI Gault, US Army.)** *Above:* **Sergeant Donald McMains—as he was, at Dau Tieng in 1968, while contemplating a letter home. He was killed in action in August 1969. (Photo by Bill Noyes.)**

Michael Wittmuss, who had spent his tour as a medic, left Vietnam in December of 1969. He came home in uniform and no one ever spat at him or called him a 'baby killer,' although he recalled that he did get a few dirty looks from some people. He re-enlisted again several months later and finally got his wish: he became a medical photographer, and he stayed in that field until he retired 19 years later.

'I've known some 'Nam vets that still go into a rage if you mention the war protesters, the people that went to Canada, the draft card burners or the guys that stayed in college,' Wittmuss recalled. 'I used to hate them too, but not any more. I decided that you can't go through life bearing a big hate for something for the rest of your life. It's strange how that war still keeps popping up in the news every once in a while. A couple of days ago, I was watching a TV talk show where Jane Fonda finally declared that she now regretted some of the statements she had made during the Vietnam War.

'The conflicts of that war have not yet subsided, and the healing process still continues.'

Above: **Michael 'Doc' Wittmuss, modelling some of his combat medic gear, previous to patrol duty near An Hoa, in 1969. After the photo session, he added to his ensemble: four bandoliers stuffed with surgical dressings, a flak jacket, an engineer's bag full of medical supplies, four water canteens, a field pack and other items essential to the 'mobile emergency ward' that any good corpsman had to emulate in a combat zone. (Photo courtesy of Michael Wittmuss.) Photos *at right:* South Vietnamese children, whose future hung in the balance with the war. (Photos by M Heacox via Bill Noyes.)**

Doug Condit left the Battalion Aid Station and 7th Engineers *one day* prior to his flight, 'so I wouldn't miss it!

'It was scary,' he recalled. 'I checked in at Da Nang transit, secured my possessions and went to the movie on Freedom Hill in Da Nang. There was a quarry right behind the theatre, and in order to get some rock out of it, some Marines blasted it—while I was in the theatre! I thought we were getting attacked with rockets!

'I had a quick flight to Okinawa, but then had to spend nine days there while waiting for a plane back to the world. As I was E5, I only had to make muster every morning, to see when we would be leaving. No other responsibilities. While on Okinawa, I met Larry Spencer, a friend of mine from the ambulance company back home in Denver. He and all the people going over looked so pale and anemic. I told Larry a slogan I heard in 'Nam: "For those who fight for it, life has a flavor the protected will never know." When I returned to Denver from Okinawa, I stopped by to see Larry's dad, Father Spencer, an Episcopalian priest, and tell him that I'd seen Larry. He was honestly pleased that I had made it through my tour in 'Nam. He had received a tape from Larry, and Larry had included my phrase on it. He asked from whence it came. I told him that it was written in/on most out-houses in

Above: **The 25th Infantry Division GI known as 'Teach' takes a break by Highway 239 during a road sweep in 1969. (Photo by Bill Noyes.)** *At right:* **Members of the First Cavalry Division on Operation Lincoln, in the Chu Pong Mountain Range in April, 1966. (Photo by Sp5 Allan Holm, US Army.)**

These pages: Crewmen of the Amphibious command ship USS *Blue Ridge* push a South Vietnamese UH-1 Huey into the sea. Several South Vietnamese pilots had landed on the ship for refuge, and their aircraft had to be pushed into the sea to make room on deck for other refugees escaping from the mainland. It was 28 April 1975 — the US Embassy had been evacuated, Saigon had fallen and the people of South Vietnam were fleeing in panic and confusion in the face of the North Vietnamese onslaught.

This had been predicted years earlier, when America withdrew its combat troops in 1973 — upon the signing of the Paris agreement, and achievement of US President Richard Nixon's 'peace with honor.' For the South Vietnamese, however, after 30 years and three major conflicts in their country, there was to be no respite. In January of 1975, the North Vietnamese Army began its drive south, and achieved its conquest of South Vietnam in four months. (Photo by Ph3 M Musser, US Navy.)

'Nam. Fortunately, Larry came home shortly, due to some kind of illness within his family, and he did not have to return or fulfill a year in 'Nam!

'I guess we had a role there, but I guess political leaders blew it. *If* a country has to have over half a million men in a war, you would think that the country would allow them to win it. However, both sides fought dumb! In grade school, one learns the adage: "A chain is only as strong as its weakest link." America's weakest link was bodies. Americans had a tough time hearing body counts on the nightly news. So this is where we hit the North Vietnamese—by counting their bodies, which they had plenty of! Their weakest link was supplies—especially expensive ones— which we didn't try to cut off until the war had wound down and Nixon had us retreating. Meanwhile, the North Vietnamese were trying to do away with *our* expensive equipment. Yet every time they'd shoot a copter out of the sky, we'd bring in another the next day from Okinawa or the Philippines. Both sides *struck the other at their strongest link*.

'I imagine that the war could have been won, *if* we had struck Hanoi at the beginning and done away with the Hanoi government. Otherwise, I guess the war was pretty much predestined to come out the the way it did—with us on the losing end. While I wish America would chastise the politicians for getting us in such a mess, the men who went there—who fought there and died there— are no less heroes than those who died for America in any previous war. Even today, I do not honestly know how I feel about our involvement there. After all, Senator J William Fulbright—who was a Rhodes Scholar—said we should go.'

Above: **This Vietnamese village girl, though photographed in 1968, seems to contemplate the scene** *below*: **a villager, shot by accident in Viet Cong/ARVN crossfire, is brought to an aid station by his wife in 1962. (Above photo by Bill Noyes.)** *At right:* **The average GI, on whose shoulders the war rested.**

BACK WITH A VENGEANCE

By Aaron Zeff

Two more minutes before the opening of small game season, Vince thought. I've just returned from Vietnam and this is the first time I'll be hunting again.

The season starts off with the blasting of shotguns at rabbits, pheasants and other small game. Over three dozen hunters converge in a relatively small area and begin blasting away.

Guns, guns, war, Vietnam, death, blasting away, blasting away. First week home, gone hunting, blasting away…

Vince shudders.

That blasting… we're being overrun! It's happening so quick. What if I'm captured? Will I obey the military Code of Conduct? My instructor's voice echoes in my mind: 'Repeat after me, I am an American fighting man.' I get goose pimples. I never thought about how important it was to be a Marine non-commissioned officer. I had enlisted, but I never thought I'd be here fighting in this stinking place. Those damn radicals at home. These damn guys over here. Can't they ever follow an order? I told them to dig bunkers, not shit holes. I…

'Hey, Vince, you gonna hunt or screw around?'

'What?'

'C'mon, let's get some bunnies, and later we'll take a break, get some coffee, shoot a little pool.'

'Good. Let's go.'

The red and yellow sign read 'C-2 Washout Area. Open For Business. All Are Welcome.' A mud-colored stream, surrounded by pock-marked and burned mountains, serving as guardians of death that still linger, show scant clues of what has happened. Bobbing behind a bush are the fragmented remains of a green helmet. On the bank, which once held laughing men, lay grotesque reminders of what was alive and is now dead: a shattered pair of glasses, a bloody pair of pants and a bent sergeant's chevron.

'Get 'em, Vince! Hey, what the hell's wrong with you? You gonna hunt, or what?'

'I don't know, Rob. I just can't seem to get with it. Shit, all this firing makes me think I'm in 'Nam again.'

'Do you want to go back to the car?'

'No, not yet. I don't want to screw you guys up. Let me just walk a little by myself. I'll be able do it if I go a little slower. I'll still get something. Slow or fast, I still know how to hunt.'

'Just watch that you don't get something like shot. I don't want to look for a new hunting partner.'

'Yeah.'

I hope to hell I'll be able to get Vietnam off my mind. That's all I need, to crack up now that I'm finally home. I sure thought that I would end up in the nut house in Vietnam—all that noise. If it wasn't for me getting that shit assin' malaria and going to the hospital for a month, I think my mind would have exploded. Those mortars every day and night, thump, thump, thump, and hardly any sleep. Those gooks, if only they would hit us during the day. Always when it was dark. That's okay. Our planes shook them out of their holes when it got light. As soon as it got a little lighter outside, that spotter glided over, dropped some smoke, and the number of gooks was reduced.

Those mortars, I just couldn't get used to them. Sixteen men wounded last month because of a mortar. Because they goofed around, they wounded their own. It seems

At left: **Soldiers of the 25th Infantry Division get ready for a sortie at the base camp in Dau Tieng. (Photo by Bill Noyes.)**

ironic. We finally survived a month of steady fighting, finally got a chance to move back into a little safer area— and shit! We get it. One short round, one round that fell short because some goof-off didn't check his mortar. As the base plate that holds the mortar in place sank into the ground from the constant firing, the mortar tube was drawn into the air. The arc of the missile was shortened and it fell into friendly territory. Just when we got a chance to get cleaned up, one round fell in the stream and wounded sixteen of us.

And me, one piece of shrapnel pierced the skin on my leg and I froze. One small second I froze—just long enough to be killed if another mortar would have come in. The screaming of a man on the bank snapped me back to reality. His back was covered with blood; his hands were over his head, grasping at air. Instinctively, I ran to his aid.

'Hey, take it easy. It's only a small hole! The blood is mixing with the water on your back and it just looks bad. Look, get your clothes on and walk over to sick bay. Shit on your rifle. I'll take care of it.'

All that blood and screaming. 'Corpsman! Corpsman up! Corpsman!' For over an hour we helped the wounded and searched for dead bodies. My conscious mind did not control my body any more; I moved by reflex. We couldn't have done that if not for the continuous training we had

At top and middle: **American GIs with captured Viet Cong munitions during the Tet Offensive.** *Above:* **An American underground bunker. (Photos by Jack Casper via Bill Noyes.)** *At right:* **An American machine gunner fires a burst during a 'shoot and duck' firefight with North Vietnamese Army troops.**

received before we went there. Everywhere we went—left, right, left, right, column of files to the right, to the rear march—and all that other shit, till we hated it, until it was part of us.

I now look upon those hated days and am thankful—without that training, I couldn't have possibly survived. Those constant marches till my legs felt like jelly and the pain in my shins that shot up my legs until they became unbearable. The straps from my pack that dug into and rubbed my shoulders until I felt like giving up. But give up—no! When the pain becomes so intolerable, that's the time to dig in; that's when quitting is unheard of. Many times I said to myself: just a little more, just a little more. Each little more brought me closer to success, and each ounce of pain helped me to survive. Each memory that stayed etched in my brain added to my chances of coming home from Vietnam alive and with a clear conscience that I had not let anyone else die. Without that training, how could I have survived all that I did?

Maybe I ought to go back to the car. Rob's right. Maybe I will get shot. My mind just isn't in the right place. I don't think I'll do any more hunting this year. I'll have to see what happens next year, if I can forget about Vietnam. At least I haven't had nightmares about it. What else would I need?

Sitting in the car with the firing outside makes me feel like we are going into combat again. Closing my eyes, I can see our helicopter taking off, combat troops on the ground crouched low to avoid the debris hurtled at them by the wind-making propeller. In seconds these men seem to shrink and are shortly out of sight.

Glittering in the sun, silver quonset huts stand as gateways to the war. Replacing the glitter, the dark treetops form a canopy to hide the enemy. Occasionally the jungle opens and reveals the acne-like texture of the ground, the result of bombs dropped to rid the enemy of more of its population. Passing over Hill 881, I saw the history of Vietnam—ravaged, scarred, and stripped of its dignity. None of us are really scared yet. Just another Marine Corps game—until the gunners on our helicopter begin to fire. It is real! We are going to offer our lives as sacrifices; some of us were taken up on it.

I learned a lot about myself and what it's like to be in charge of Hill 881. The Viet Cong gave me all the opportunities. The first day we got mortared with a vengeance. I sat in my hole with three of my men, watching, listening and praying. I saw men cry, and I couldn't. I had to keep it inside. I couldn't let my men think that I was scared. I had to make the jokes. The Viet Cong were well aware of the fears we American fighting men have. If we let our fear get the best of us, the gooks will walk right in and drop grenades on us.

Not in our hole, though. We took turns looking—

Above: **US Army personnel, in an encounter with the enemy. The soldier in the middle is armed with a grenade launcher.** *At right:* **A trooper of the 173rd Airborne takes cover in a firefight during Operation Greeley in 1968.**

Above: **A Huey at sunset. New troops usually first tasted real danger when the helicopter bringing them to the battle zone drew ground fire. (Photo by David Bowman.)** *At right:* **A night mortar attack at Hue during the Tet Offensive. Seasoned soldiers found the nearest cover at the sound of incoming rounds.**

looking to make sure that we were really being mortared and not merely being tricked into thinking we were. We have to think we are getting overrun and pray that we aren't. Some of these boots think they know it all. Young punks, just getting over here, and they think they got it all figured out. They think they can go to classes, read their books and become good fighting men. The only think they know how to do is get themselves killed. What do they know of the devious tricks these North Vietnamese have? Tricks like whistles that sound like mortars so that they can run in and grenade us. These young hoodlums have probably never seen a man shot and killed, a bullet hole maybe ripping out a stomach or taking part of a head with it. Hah! I remember when I first got here. I was just as stupid as they are. The first time we got mortared, I didn't know whether to run, laugh or cry. Yeah, they laughed at me for awhile.

'Hey, boot, get in this hole!'

'I can't. There's too many guys in there.'

'Shit, just jump in. You'll make it safer for the ones on the bottom!'

How could I have been so dumb? The other guys knew what to do. There was no hesitation from them. They just jumped into the closest hole available to them and nobody asked any questions. And afterward, when it came to digging foxholes, I was right on it. I never thought I'd dig holes and like it. These guys will be doing it, too. I'll see some good holes and bunkers tomorrow. Each of us here are going through the hardest of educations—the school of experience—and the tuition is our bodies and graduation is our life or death.

I'm glad to be out of that place. I can't see why anyone would want to stay longer than he had to. All of those guys that extended for six more months. I can see wanting to do your job while being there, but to stay—no, I just can't see it.

Maybe I'm no better, though. The time I had malaria and wouldn't stay in the hospital for the required time. That was a good lie I formulated to get back. I had R&R to Hawaii to see my wife and kids. What R&R? What wife and kids? It worked, though, and I got to go back. I must have been nuts, but I felt an obligation. Every time a new man takes over in Vietnam, it is the same: learning and making mistakes. It's only natural, but mistakes here can be hell.

Like when I first got here. Our platoon commander gave us an ambush site that was already occupied by another squad. All I remember of that night was crawling, staring at a machine gun spewing red streaks and then falling down a hole. Thank God those guys heard us yell. If they hadn't hollered, 'Are you Americans?' we would have had a real firefight between us. That mistake caused the loss of one man's eye. A stupid, bitchin' mistake by some boot-assed lieutenant. I guess those guys that stayed were stupid, but...

The man that replaced me was good and had been there before. I wonder how those guys made out? I'm afraid to write; I'd hate to find out they are dead.

Yes, I sure would like to know what happened to GD Miller, Lusch, Lightning and Raymond. I owe those guys a lot. I hope they made it back. If it wasn't for them being my friends, I don't think that I would have made it back. How can I ever repay them? At least I was able to recommend Lusch for a Silver Star and Miller for Corporal. What's that, though? No, I can never repay them. They did the work and I got the credit. I looked good because my men were good. What made Lusch man a position by himself? What made those men understand and volunteer when I had to take a night patrol out and was afraid that they would get killed? I skipped over them, but they didn't see that.

They'll be in my mind for the rest of my life. Some day I'll try to look them up, and until then, I'll think they made it.

I'd like to hear from Captain Allan, too. Not many people like him. Not many people knew why he was so hard on us. No one knew why he demanded perfection. People that had known him before said he was different. The last time he had been there, he had lost a lot of men. Most of his men got on one helicopter and he and a few others got on another. The first one was shot down and every man aboard was killed.

He never forgave himself. He was a true leader, though, and gave me much inspiration and determination not to make mistakes. I hope none of his own men killed him.

Let me open a few windows in this car. I can't stand being closed up for too long. I can't see how I survived living in a bunker at Con Tien for three months. No room, no air, and everything full of mildew. And, to top it off, every time we went outside, we had to wear a helmet and flack jacket even to shave. That lieutenant from D Company almost had kittens the time he caught me without my helmet on while shaving.

'Hey, Marine! Get that helmet on!' I looked up, but without my glasses on, I couldn't see who it was. I figured, who the hell is this guy telling me to put my helmet on?

Then he said, 'Hey, Marine. Get over here!'

I went to see who it was and saw that it was the Lieutenant. He bawled me out. When I turned around, I said, 'Get laid.'

'What?' he said. He was so pissed off, his lower lip began to tremble.

I put my helmet on. I'm just glad he stayed in D Company.

'Hey, Vince, look what we got! Two bunnies and a ringneck. You about ready for that coffee?'

'No, but let's go. I'm tired of hunting.'

At right: **Monks walk a path near Dau Tieng in 1968. (Photo by Bill Noyes.)**

EPILOGUE

Erich Maria Remarque closed *All Quiet On The Western Front* with words which could easily stand as a tribute to the men and women who served in Vietnam:

It is autumn. There are not many of the old hands left. I am the last of the seven fellows from our class.

Everyone talks of peace and armistice. All wait. If it again proves an illusion, then they will break up; hope is high, it cannot be taken away again without an upheaval. If there is not peace, then there will be revolution.

I have fourteen days rest, because I have swallowed a bit of gas; in a little garden I sit the whole day long in the sun. The armistice is coming soon, I believe it now too. Then we will go home.

Here my thoughts stop and will not go any farther. All that meets me, all that floods over me are but feelings — greed of life, love of home, yearning of the blood, intoxication of deliverance. But no aims.

Had we returned home in 1916, out of the suffering and the strength of our experience we might have unleashed a storm. Now if we go back we will be weary, broken, burnt out, rootless, and without hope. We will not be able to find our way any more.

And men will not understand us—for the generation that grew up before us, though it has passed these years with us here, already had a home and a calling; now it will return to its old occupations, and the war will be forgotten—and the generation that has grown up after us will be strange to us and push us aside. We will be superfluous even to ourselves, we will grow older, a few will adapt themselves, some others will merely submit, and most will be bewildered;—the years will pass by and in the end we shall fall into ruin.

But perhaps all this that I think is mere melancholy and dismay, which will fly away as the dust, when I stand once again beneath the poplars and listen to the rustling of their leaves. It cannot be that it has gone, the yearning that made our blood unquiet, the unknown, the perplexing, the oncoming things, the thousand faces of the future, the melodies from dreams and from books, the whispers and divinations of women, it cannot be that this has vanished in bombardment, in despair, in brothels.

Here the trees show gay and golden, the berries of the rowan stand red among the leaves, country roads run white out to the sky-line, and the canteens hum like beehives with rumors of peace.

I stand up.

I am very quiet. Let the months and years come, they bring me nothing more, they can bring me nothing more. I am so alone, and so without hope that I can confront them without fear. The life that has borne me through these years is still in my hands and my eyes. Whether I have subdued it, I know not. But so long as it is there it will seek its own way out, heedless of the will that is within me.

*   *   *

He fell in October 1918, on a day that was so quiet and still on the whole front, that the army report confined itself to the single sentence: All quiet on the Western Front.

He had fallen forward and lay on the earth as though sleeping. Turning him over one saw that he could not have suffered long; his face had an expression of calm, as though almost glad the end had come.

At right: The statue of Vietnam-era American ground troops that overlooks the Vietnam Memorial in Washington, DC. The men and women who fought and served in Vietnam gave much for their country, and in retrospect it can be said that the building of a memorial to their fallen comrades was a fitting, but somehow inadequate, gesture to honor the gallantry of the many who *did* return from that extraordinary war.

In many ways, theirs was a thankless task. While numerous Vietnam veterans have gone on to successful careers and full, fruitful lives, our contemporary popular media focuses on the ones who were not so fortunate.

This belated and all-too-necessary concern leads to the thought that, probably, the greatest defeat that the United States has suffered in *any* war was the failure to overcome the attitude of coldness, and indifference, with which Americans shunned most of those returning veterans. Let us never forget the men and women who served our country so valiantly and at such a cost—in the difficult, much-repudiated and unforgettable Vietnam War.

Page 192: The sun sets over the South China Sea, in this view of an observation post located somewhere on the coast of South Vietnam. (Photo by Lou Graul Eisenberg.)

INDEX

BIOGRAPHIES

DAVID J BOWMAN received his induction notice the day before his 21st birthday. He entered the Army, was trained as a combat infantryman, and served in Vietnam from September 1967 until September 1968 with the 1st Battalion, 8th Cavalry of the First Cavalry Division (Airmobile). He then spent 15 years with the San Francisco Police Department, including seven years as a TAC Squad (SWAT Team) officer and another seven years as a detective. He now lives in a small village on the mid-coast of Maine with his wife and six-year-old son.

DOUGLAS CONDIT, JR, who entered the Navy from Glenwood Springs, Colorado, served as a Marine Corps corpsman with the Second Battalion, 27th Marines and with the Seventh Engineers in Vietnam in 1968 and 1969. After receiving civilian refining of his medical knowledge, he presently lives and works as a cardiothoracic physician assistant in New York City.

LOU GRAUL EISENBRANDT, an Army nurse, worked in the emergency room of the 91st Evacuation Hospital in Chu Lai from November 1969 to November 1970. She presently lives and works as a travel agent in Overland Park, Kansas. She is married and has a daughter and a son.

REVEREND SAMUEL L HOARD (Colonel, USA, Ret), then a Captain, served as a chaplain with the 1st Battalion, Eighth Cavalry of the First Cavalry Division (Airmobile) at An Khe from May 1967 until May 1968. He is now the pastor of Our Savior Lutheran Church in Orlando, Florida.

BILL NOYES served with B Company, Second Battalion, 22d Infantry, 25th Infantry Division during 1968 and 1969. He currently lives and works in Campbell, California.

GARY P WILLIAMS served in Vietnam with B Company, 2d Battalion, 60th Infantry. He currently lives and works in Rome, New York.

MICHAEL A WITTMUSS enlisted in the Navy in March, 1966 and served as a Navy medic in Vietnam in 1968 and 1969. After his return home, he continued his military career as a medical photographer until his retirement on 29 February 1988. He now lives and works in Carlsbad, California.

AARON ZEFF, born and now living in Pittsburgh, Pennsylvania, is married with two daughters. He served in Vietnam in 1967 and 1968 with the 1st Battalion, Fourth Marines as a squad leader and platoon sergeant, based at Dong Ha and later moving below the DMZ. The unit then left Con Tien to help relieve the siege of Khe Sanh. After serving in the Marine Corps, Mr Zeff graduated from the University of Pittsburgh, and is now the owner and president of Delta Trading Corporation, a company that brokers a diversity of products, including pizza crusts, plastic bags, food products, coal and steel.

ML

12/02